Praise for

BECOMING
flawesome

"Kristina Mänd-Lakhiani takes us on an inward
journey toward authenticity, with the conviction that
positive change within and without can only come from
there. Reading her book, I was reminded of the secret revealed
by the Little Prince, that what is essential cannot be seen with
the eyes but with the heart. Here, you can learn to experience
who you really are and how to accept that genuine person,
using well thought-out exercises and bearing in mind
that it all begins simply by practising awareness."

— **Princess Rym Ali**, president of the Anna Lindh Foundation

"Full of timely wisdom for those
who want to live their perfectly imperfect life."

— **Jim Kwik**, *New York Times* best-selling author of *Limitless*

"A road map to deep self-awareness,
radical self-acceptance, and genuine self-love.
An inspiring read for any individual prepared to
embark on a journey toward their truest self."

— **Dr. Shefali**, *New York Times* bestselling author of
The Conscious Parent and clinical psychologist

"A brilliant gift for anyone who has ever
doubted their strength and power to create a life
that is unapologetically their own. Mänd-Lakhiani
inspires the courage and conviction we need to
live lives of deep integrity, joy, and truth."

— **Katherine Woodward Thomas**, *New York Times* best-selling
author of *Calling in "The One"* and *Conscious Uncoupling*

"A refreshingly honest, insightful, and liberating book . . . one which *frees* you from the prison of beliefs and values guaranteed to destroy your Spirit and gently walks you back to the safety, sanity, and lasting success of your heart."

— **Sonia Choquette**, *New York Times* best-selling author of
The Answer Is Simple . . . Love Yourself, Live Your Spirit!

"A powerful insight into the prospect of nurturing a healthy relationship with the most important person in our lives: ourselves. Beautifully written and authentically delivered, it's a must-read for anyone working on improving their self-worth."

— **Marisa Peer**, therapist and best-selling author
of *Tell Yourself a Better Lie*

"Get ready to embark on a life-changing journey with *Flawesome*—the ultimate guide to unlocking your authentic self. Kristina takes you on a journey to uncover the power of your imperfections and redefine your definition of success. A brilliant, raw, and honest exploration of the human experience that produces real transformation. Prepare to laugh, cry, and exhale with liberation as you read this book."

— **Florencia Andrés**, best-selling author of
Renuévate con confianza total, winner of the Golden Book award,
and coach of sports champions, celebrities, and CEOs

"Kristina's wisdom will guide you through a journey of self-discovery and freedom. Kristina asks questions that will not only give you insights but will help you find the beliefs that keep you stuck. This is an adventure worth taking!"

— **Shelly Lefkoe**, co-founder of the Lefkoe Institute

"*Becoming Flawesome* is like 10 years' worth of therapy in one book. I would encourage every single woman who has ever doubted herself to read this book."

— **Amy White**, editor

BECOMING
flawesome

BECOMING
flawesome

THE KEY TO LIVING AN
IMPERFECTLY AUTHENTIC LIFE

KRISTINA MÄND-LAKHIANI

HAY HOUSE, INC.
Carlsbad, California • New York City
London • Sydney • New Delhi

**Library of Congress Cataloging-in-Publication Data
is on file at the Library of Congress**

Hardcover ISBN: 978-1-4019-7434-3
E-book ISBN: 978-1-4019-7435-0
Audiobook ISBN: 978-1-4019-7436-7
10 9 8 7 6 5 4 3 2
1st edition, June 2023

SUSTAINABLE
FORESTRY
INITIATIVE
Certified Chain of Custody
Promoting Sustainable Forestry
www.sfiprogram.org
SFI-01268
SFI label applies to the text stock

Printed in the United States of America

To my family
for their unwavering love:
Eve, Hayden, Vishen, Ljubov,
Virgo, Roopi, and Mohan

Contents

LET'S
Begin

It is a truth universally acknowledged, that a good book has to start with a proper introduction. And by "proper" I mean that it has to prime the reader for the journey, raise excitement and set expectations, explain the process, and make reading the book an experience both profitable and smooth. After all, we are about to spend some time together on this journey.

Therefore, I was not surprised when on the first meeting with my publisher I was asked if I would consider writing a proper introduction to my book. You see—the original manuscript started with a story of me pondering my future book while standing in the shower, warm water running down my back, and my finger absentmindedly drawing random patterns on the fogged-up glass.

I started this book during the long years of successive COVID confinements, and I was planning to self-publish it because I wanted the freedom to make decisions about the book—how to write, what to write, what stories to include, what kind of experience to offer to my reader. So, naturally, it wasn't following any universally acknowledged truths or conventions.

Yet, by the time I had to present my book-baby to the world, I felt that I wanted to give it the best possible future, and I had to face the big decision between my heart and my brain: Will it be self-published (heart), or will I work with a traditional publisher (brain)? Going the traditional way meant facing more choices between my quirky and obstinate self-expression and conventional ways of doing things.

This book is about finding your way back to yourself, about understanding who you really are, accepting your dents and scratches, your quirky uniqueness and even your flaws. It is about thriving in being unapologetically you, most flawesomely.

This book has been through the hands of several editors ever since I put the last stop on its original manuscript. This journey has been both emotional and transformative for me. I had to face my biggest dragon by far—my obstinate need for pure self-expression—over and over again.

When do you follow convention, and when do you stick to your own principles and values?

There is no simple answer to this question, except: you have to learn to balance.

If you follow all the rules that your peers expect you to follow, you bet all there is on a slim chance of the grand prize, but you do it at the price of your own unique self-expression. At times, I felt like I had to "sell my soul to the devil" for a chance at success.

But if you obstinately stick to your own unique quirks and principles, you might end up being unheard and misunderstood so universally that there is no point in writing a book. For it is the readers who make a writer. Without the readers, a book is just a private diary.

Reader, will you judge me if I tell you that this book is a delicate balance between convention and my own uniqueness? Of course I want you to succeed. But I cannot give you the proper introduction to my book because every book is a journey. This book has been my journey, and now it is yours.

I walked my path to my true self, to understanding what makes me truly me . . . and what of that unique quirkiness is simply noise. You see, your flaws and your dragons are there for a reason—they make you who you are, but they also hold the key to your biggest value, to your mightiest strengths, if you choose to look your dragons in the eye.

Now I am hoping that you will take this journey with me to *your* unique destination—to finding the path back to *you*. I will be your companion on this journey, but it is yours to take.

So why wouldn't I tell you what's ahead? Imagine if Gandalf told Bilbo Baggins that on his journey, he would encounter trolls, go through a perilous enchanted forest, and face a dragon in a far-away mountain.[1] Wouldn't that be a bit of a spoiler?

I want you to take this journey back to you without any spoilers, with an open heart, and trust that the destination is going to be worth your effort. Because becoming flawesome is the best gift you can give to yourself.

So, if you are ready, let's begin!

PART I

THE
PATH
BACK TO
You

Authenticity
OF THE
SECOND DEGREE

The reward for conformity was that everyone liked you except yourself.

— RITA MAE BROWN[1]

"I've missed you," said my friend when I walked into the office one day. Without even thinking, I blurted out: "I missed me too!"

I said it, and suddenly, like a vinyl record that had been forcefully stopped with a screeching sound, I paused and gasped. I was missing myself. *Myself*?!

Don't get me wrong. I was fully functional and operating at 100 percent. I was showing up in the office, attending meetings, going to events and costume parties, speaking on stage, hanging out with friends, and being an engaged parent. Some even called me an *inspiration*.

But I was moving around in a fog, living my life but, actually, just whiling away the time given to me. And while my life was happening, I was missing one important ingredient—myself.

When did I slip away and move on without noticing the missing protagonist of my own movie?

I was 40 when I started suspecting that I was living a lie. Not a bad lie. Not a complete and utter lie. Just a little pretending—a mask here and there, a little playing along to fit in.

Just about . . . 5 percent of a lie. And 95 percent true.

But can one be 95 percent honest and authentic? I think that authenticity and honesty are absolutes. Authenticity is binary. You are either 100 percent authentic or you are not. And so is honesty—you are either 100 percent honest or you are not. You cannot be mostly honest. Or mostly authentic.

There is this funny exchange in one of my favourite novels by Bulgakov, *The Master and Margarita*. The exchange happens between the main antagonist, Woland, and a manager of a restaurant. Woland says that the fish in the restaurant is rotten, and the manager replies to the effect of: "It was delivered yesterday, it was second-degree fresh." To which Woland replies in the vein of: "There's only one degree of freshness—the first, which makes it also the last. If the fish is second-degree fresh, it means it's rotten."[2]

And so, by the age of 40, I was done with the "second-degree authenticity." I longed to be myself, fully, unapologetically, 100 percent.

I was lost. And I wanted to find the path back to myself.

Reflection Points

Throughout this book, I am going to invite you to pause for a moment and ask yourself questions. I call such exercises "moments of introspection." I believe that true growth is fuelled by curiosity. It is not my ideas that matter, but the questions that you ask yourself. And the first question that I invite you to ask yourself is this:

- Why did you decide to read this book?
- What made you pick up a book about becoming flawesome and living authentically? Curiosity? Advertising? Your own questions that you are trying to find answers to?
- And what do you expect to achieve by reading this book?

Your journey back to yourself is yours to take, and its success depends on how committed you are to this path.

ARE YOU *Lost?*

*Sometimes when you lose
your way, you find yourself.*

— MANDY HALE[3]

"How are the kids doing?"

I'm used to this question. It is civil and a very common way to start a conversation with someone who is a parent. I don't mind such icebreakers, and, like any parent, I like to talk about my children.

However, I know full well that people don't want to hear long accounts of how someone else's children are doing at school, about their achievements in sports or music, and other such details. Especially those without kids themselves. They are quite happy with a short summary: "Hayden is taller than me now and speaks in a deep voice. And they are doing great, of course."

Then there comes an awkward pause and the sideways tilt, their body language screaming that the conversation is over.

My kids are an important part of my life, and I love my children more than anything. I am a very engaged parent—I spend time with my kids; I ask questions; I know their friends, their events, and deadlines; I know what interests them, what they like, and what they don't like.

My kids are an important part of my life. But they are not *all* that there is in my life. I have my work, my mission. I have my company, my team. I'm a writer and an author. I have friends, and I travel the world. I have interests, and I am curious about life, politics, social issues—so many things!

Every time this used to happen to me, I would flare up internally. "Why do you only ask me about my children? Can we talk about other things? Do you know there are other things in my life that are important to me?"

And then the Good Mom in me would start shaming the Obstinate Attention-Seeker. "You love your kids. You are a good mother. What are you upset about? Are you upset that people don't know that you do other things besides mothering? How dare you feel incomplete?! Being a mother is so important. It is your ego. Shut up and be happy!"

What brilliant advice! And completely useless.

Have you ever felt guilty for what you feel? Have you ever thought that you are not supposed to feel what you feel—that it is somehow wrong or inappropriate?

"I shouldn't feel upset because of such a trifle—there is a lot of real suffering in the world."

"I shouldn't feel so worried about this situation—I know I'm just overthinking."

"I shouldn't feel so angry with this person—I choose love."

"I shouldn't feel so down for no reason—I have so much to be grateful for."

"I shouldn't feel so misunderstood for not being acknowledged—I don't need external validation."

"I shouldn't feel so excited about being praised—I don't need external validation."

"I shouldn't feel so heartbroken—this person wasn't good for me."

"I shouldn't feel so bored with my kids/friends/family—I love them."

"I shouldn't feel so bored with my work—I love what I do."

"I shouldn't feel so unmotivated—I have to cheer up."

And so it goes. You internally say, "I shouldn't feel . . ." and you fill in the blank.

How often do you tell yourself that you should be feeling something entirely different from what you are actually feeling at that moment? And when you catch yourself with an unwanted feeling, what do you do with it? Do you tell yourself how you are supposed to be feeling instead? Do you force yourself to shake it off, cheer up, get over it, and rise above it?

That is how we are used to dealing with adversity. That is what we are told. Depending on the situation, your advice might be absolutely appropriate. But good advice must come at a good time. And the timing of such advice may be a little premature when you are forcing it at a time when what you are feeling is the exact opposite.

People have a funny tendency to brush over the unpleasant and the uncomfortable, and to rush straight into how it is supposed to be in a perfect world. And if we don't have the skill to deal with the unpleasant and the uncomfortable, we try to push through it, rush over to the other side, and force it out of our system. We make ourselves feel bad for what we feel—this is how we lose ourselves.

You cannot shame and guilt yourself out of what you feel. It doesn't work like that. We'll go deeper into unwanted feelings and how to deal with them in Part IV of this book. Meanwhile, let's come back to our original question: How did you become a missing person in your own life?

Reflection Points

Over the next few days, pay attention to your thoughts and catch yourself whenever you think that what you are feeling is somehow "wrong." Ask yourself these questions:

- What am I feeling right now?
- What do I not like about this feeling?
- What would I like to feel instead?
- How does this contradiction make me feel?

You can start a journal and write down all your realisations at the end of each day. It will help you get clarity, integrate new ideas, and get unlost by becoming better at recognising how you really feel.

LIVING WITH
Perfectionism,
AKA HERMIONE SYNDROME

Have no fear of perfection— you'll never reach it.

— SALVADOR DALÍ[4]

Hermione, the overachieving best friend of Harry Potter, is level-headed, logical, and always does the right thing—the ultimate "good" girl. *Hermione Syndrome* is not a medical or scientific term. I came up with it because I used to suffer from it. And I still do, occasionally.

I am an only child, born in the Soviet Union at the height of its idealistic and utopian existence. So my natural desire to be "good" (and we are all born good and grow up wanting to be good) was on steroids.

First, I am the only hope of my parents, and I have no room for error—there is no smarter, better sibling to do the right thing. It's all on me. Second, Soviet society was incredibly idealistic and prudish, and individuals were to be in the service of the common good of all people. So naturally, the pressure to be good was overwhelming.

Humans want to be good. We might define the idea of being good differently, but we strive to be good. In fact, we strive to be better. Or to be factually more accurate, we strive to be more of what we think is the perfect version of ourselves: The Perfect Me.

Have you ever fallen in love with the idea of someone rather than the real person?[5] I'm sure you must have. We all do that to a degree. It is a natural tendency of our brain to downplay warning signs, and even red flags, and emphasise ideal qualities of our love interest while we are falling for them. (Apparently, we get to thank our evolutionary need to reproduce for this little inconvenience.)

As a result, we fall in love with an idea that we have in our head—a picture of perfection—not a *real* person. For one, the actual person probably is trying their best to be liked by you. Plus our brain doesn't like gaps, and we fill in the blanks with our own imagination if we don't have enough information. And so, after a little romance and mutual flirtation, we end up in love with a figment of our imagination that does not exist in real life.

Now what if we apply the same idea to your most important relationship—the relationship with yourself?

Whether consciously or not, you have an ideal picture of a Perfect You in your head. Just like with a love partner, it is a list of traits and qualities that make you the best version of you, worthy of love and admiration. And just like with a love partner, this idea is just a figment of your imagination, which does not (yet) exist in real life.

In love, when the period of infatuation is over and we descend down to Earth from Cloud Nine, we start seeing the real person in our love partner. Hopefully, we still love the real person. But it is not uncommon to feel a little disillusioned when we realise that we have fallen in love with an idea, not the actual human being.

The same happens in your most important relationship too. When you realise the difference between the Real You and the Perfect You, you might feel a little disillusioned. Maybe even disappointed.

And that, I believe, is why so many people struggle with self-love and self-acceptance. Because the object of their self-love is an idea in their heads. That version of themselves doesn't actually exist yet. And the further that idea is from the Real You, the harder it is to love yourself.

I've been a "perfect girl" all my life. I studied well. I behaved well, didn't cause any trouble. I went to a good university and got a great degree. I found an amazing job while I was still studying and made a great career for myself within the Estonian government by my early 20s. At 25, I was wondering what to do with the rest of my life—the president of Estonia by 30, and then what?

I took all the right steps, living by the book, following the path to great success. By the age of 40, I had a successful business, a husband, two children (a boy and a girl); I was traveling the world and living a perfectly Instagrammable life. It was the height, the peak of my Hermione Syndrome—a perfect woman in a perfect setting.

The only place where I could let my hair down—where I could break down and cry, where I could admit that I was lost and confused—was the bathroom, behind the locked door. Naturally. Because I couldn't ruin the perfect picture of The Perfect Me by admitting publicly (well, even just among my closest family) that I wasn't as perfect as I tried to look.

Perfectionism is a terrible burden. We adopt it out of the best intentions because we *want* to be good; we want to be seen as someone who doesn't make mistakes, who has life figured out, who is flawless. But it is the one thing that often stands between us and real, lasting, deep happiness and the feeling of peace and fulfilment.

You might say, "Isn't it good to strive to be a better version of me?" My poor Hermione, you are right—of course it is good. But you cannot become a better version of you, or any version of you for that matter, until you come to peace and accept the *current* version of you.

You see, transformation does not happen out of thin air. It's more like hiking with a map. While you might know where you want to go, you will not be able to use the map unless you know where you start the hike from—your current location.

It is my hope that this book, as a side effect, will help you heal your Hermione Syndrome and give up perfectionism once and for all.

Reflection Points

In the next few days, pay attention to the moments when your perfectionist streak manifests:

- You might feel discontent because something is not to your liking, not perfect.
- You might feel anxious or overwhelmed because you want to appear to be perfect.
- You might feel stuck because your idea of perfection is overwhelming.
- You might feel the need to perform a task perfectly.

When you catch yourself in such moments, stop, take a deep breath, and then give yourself permission *not* to be perfect. Do it just for a few days and notice how it makes you feel. You can get back to being perfect after a day or two if you find imperfection too stressful.

Success
IS NOT
THE DESTINATION

*Success is as ice cold
and lonely as the North Pole.*

— VICKI BAUM[6]

It is curious how rigid we can be in our concept of success. For one, it is usually measured in monetary value. Typically, in Western capitalistic societies, we are trained to equate financial achievements to overall success. Thus the affluent may seem happier, healthier, more beautiful, and more accomplished at whichever task they undertake.

What success means may vary from place to place and depend on the circumstances—a successful Soviet citizen is a different creature from a successful American. But in general terms, we understand success similarly within the bounds of society.

For example, in most Western countries, a lean, youthful body is a measure of success when it comes to female beauty (and health, which is probably both arguable and concerning). Among the Achuar people of the Amazon rainforest, a female with a defined round belly is considered beautiful. It is so prominent a feature that you will notice little girls arching their backs and pushing their bellies forward in an effort to look more beautiful.

Not only are the cultural definitions of success clear and rigid, but the bar keeps being pushed higher and higher. For example, at the end of the 20th century, a healthy person was eating a balanced diet and leading an active lifestyle—moving sufficiently and maybe doing a bit of sport. Now you need to be an expert in nutrition, a master chef, and exercise daily (on par with professionals) to be considered a success in the area of health and fitness. Just having a healthy lifestyle will not cut it anymore.

The same goes for financial success, your life mission, your career—our demands and expectations are higher than ever. And most of us will have to face a harrowing choice in at least one area of life—the choice between being "successful" or doing what makes us happy. And those two scenarios may be contradictory.

- You might have to choose between studying law or business versus studying art or something just as "impractical." Your parents might say that going into law will make you successful, while being an artist will never be a "real job" or earn you enough money.

- You might have to choose between getting married and starting a family versus focusing on your passion or your career. This one is tough because some people expect both boxes to be ticked to be considered a success.

- You might have to choose between a promising stable career versus doing your own craft. (Many people value corporate careers above small entrepreneurship or freelancing.) And you might be facing a dilemma—your definition of success versus something that makes you genuinely happy.

My bet is that most of us will choose success over happiness. Not consciously. We'll choose success with logic: "I'm not thinking straight here. I should be logical. Success is definitely a more reasonable and responsible choice. Following one's heart, following one's passion, doing what you love, is a huge gamble!" We don't like to gamble because we want certainty. And while success sounds like a hard path, at least its destination is certain.

We choose success over happiness, not because we value success more, but because we need certainty—and we believe that happiness will be a natural consequence of success.

As I'm writing this book, I am painfully aware that if I don't hit the bestsellers list in at least one category on at least one platform—be it even the most obscure platform and the least populated category—I will not dare to consider myself a success as an author and a writer. I don't think I've yet presented any established author of a book without a pretext of "best-selling." Isn't that a little intense for a standard?

Success, we can clearly define. Yet when we think about happiness, quite sadly, the story is not as simple and clear. For the past several years, I've been reading books on happiness, listening to TED talks on happiness, digging my nose into empirical evidence and research about happiness. And if there is one conclusion I can make after all of this studying and research, it is that there is no clear definition of happiness.

Various researchers have discovered that happiness is not a side effect of success. It is quite the reverse: success is achieved more easily if you strive for it in a state of happiness.[7] In other words, success might actually be a side effect of happiness, not the other way around.

Think about it. We place success on a pedestal, we prioritise it over everything else, and we do it with one goal in mind: to be happy at the end of this gruelling race. We strive for success to be happy. So the ultimate goal is happiness. But the priority is on success: happiness is often secondary in our daily plans because we believe that it is success that will make us happy.

Yet there is overwhelming evidence that success doesn't lead to happiness. It doesn't create happiness. It may, but there is no correlation—your measure of success is not a predictor of your level of happiness.

We often think that the path to happiness lies in success. It is a cultural axiom we don't often challenge. And this axiom, this delusion, is why so many of us suffer from Hermione Syndrome, from perfectionism, and why we are so harsh toward ourselves, so self-critical, and find it hard to accept ourselves the way we are. Because ultimately, we want to be happy, but we believe that the path to happiness lies through success, and success, naturally, requires perfection.

Unfortunately, most people discover this simple error after(!) they have put in the effort, time, and resources into chasing success, *after* they have reached the top and achieved their big dreams. It is on the top of Mount Olympus[8] when you are left alone with the ultimate truth . . . and your demons for company.

I'd like to paraphrase an idea I learned from one of my favourite teachers, a famous psychotherapist and a dear friend, Marisa Peer.[9] She works with top achievers, some of the most successful people in the world, and here's what she has to say about striving for success (in my own words):

People strive for success because they think that by achieving it, they will become lovable and worthy. But they are already worthy and lovable. And when they reach success, all that happens is that they are deprived of the one motivation that has been pulling them forward toward success— the desire to feel worthy and lovable. And they are left one-on-one with themselves, with their insecurities, with their problems, which they were hoping to solve in all the wrong ways—by striving for success.

We, as a society, fail to define happiness. And not surprisingly, we have a hard time measuring and optimising it. But we'll dig into happiness a little later. For now, let me suggest this one idea as a raw theory:

Every person understands happiness in their own unique way.

Happiness is a personal phenomenon. Naturally, there may be a billion versions of happiness on planet Earth, each a little different from another.

But if happiness is a destination unique to each person, then why are we told to follow the same exact map?

Reflection Points

Today I want to ask you to make two lists. But you'll make them in the reverse order. If normally you place success first and happiness second, for this mental exercise, I want you to start with happiness.

- Make a list with your own definition of happiness: What makes you happy? How do you define happiness?

- Now make a list of what success means to you: How do you define success? How do you know that you are successful?

Finally, see how much, if at all, those lists overlap. Do they match up, or, more importantly, do they contradict in any of the points?

THE
MYTH OF
Hustling

Now, here, you see, it takes all the running you can do,
to keep in the same place. If you want to get somewhere else,
you must run at least twice as fast as that!

— LEWIS CARROLL[10]

When you are trying to follow a map, you can walk into the woods and get lost, make a few rounds, end up next to a beautiful stream and come across a deer, and then find your way out again. It wouldn't be too bad if you enjoyed the walk, if your detour was as beautiful as your destination, would it?

The real problem is that most of us don't enjoy the journey to our desired destination.

Over the years, I have interviewed hundreds of successful people from all walks of life. One mother of a successful world-class junior chess player told me: "Of course, my daughter was like any other kid. She wanted to stay in bed late on Sundays and play games all day with her friends. But I would tell her: 'You have to work and keep working hard. While everyone else is lazy, sleeping in bed, you gain your advantage, you strive for your goals.'"[11]

Western society idolises hustling. It's a status symbol. Our faith in hard work and hustling is so profound that if we find any evidence to the contrary, if success comes easy, we become suspicious—something is just not right.

"Maybe this is not a true lasting success, because 'easy' cannot be sustainable."

"Maybe I was just lucky, and luck is not replicable."

"Maybe people will soon discover that I didn't do anything to deserve my success."

"Maybe I'm not working hard enough, and I will lose it all as easily as I got it."

Do any of these internal dialogues sound familiar?

Given that up to 82 percent of successful, accomplished people suffer from impostor syndrome[12] and, according to various studies, up to 32 percent of employees in Europe suffer from burnout,[13] at least one of these thought processes probably does sound familiar to most of us.

What's more, a lot of my entrepreneur friends and colleagues feel guilty for taking a break from the hustle. They feel unproductive on holidays. They fear that a moment of rest is a waste of time. What's even worse, they often feel that time spent not working will cost them money and lost opportunities.

I was attending a mastermind event of female entrepreneurs and was shocked to hear women calling themselves lazy, unproductive, and failures for having a forced break in their working schedule. And let me tell you this: rest is not lazy, a break is not a step backward, a holiday is not stagnation, and waiting is not losing.

I want to suggest that you pick your labels and definitions very carefully.

As one of our amazing Mindvalley teachers, Eric Edmeades, put it: "A belief is a virus that feeds on evidence." In more scientific terms, a network of neurons in your brain stem—your reticular activating system[14]—is responsible for filtering out which kind of stimuli will activate your cerebral cortex. The reticular activating system is a gatekeeper deciding which of the external stimuli are important and should be passed on for you to respond to, and which are irrelevant and can be ignored.

Consequently, your goal will define your perception, since your goal will determine the relevance of external stimuli.

Let us do a little mental exercise to illustrate this concept—if you have done this exercise before at some personal growth event, just play along a bit; it is a great exercise to repeat.

Look around you right now and notice every brown object in your surroundings.

Ready? Got it? Good!

Now close your eyes and recall every green object in your environment.

Now look around once again and notice all the green objects. Did you miss anything when you were recalling green objects with your eyes closed?

It is an incredibly simple exercise to illustrate that your goal will define your perception. You will see clearly only that which you are looking for.

When you were looking for brown objects, your brain likely registered everything brown and brushed over all other objects. When I asked you to recall green objects, you might have remembered some more prominent green objects or recalled objects familiar to you, but you may not have remembered smaller, less prominent details. In fact, the task may have seemed very challenging, and rightly so, because you were not focusing on green in the first place.

Our beliefs work the same way. If we have a certain belief, we'll keep noticing proof that validates our belief and brush over any contradictions. Thus the proof that we are seeking will make us more certain in our belief and keep feeding the cycle of noticing more proof and ignoring more contradictions. It doesn't even matter if you are conscious of your belief—the reticular activating system works even with our subconscious programmes.

And so, for example, when someone tells me that success has to be earned with hard work and sacrifice, I believe them, because that is how it is going to be for them. They will see proof of this belief everywhere. Better yet, they will become the living, breathing proof of this belief.

Your beliefs spill over into your behaviour and your experience of this life. If you believe that success requires hard work and sacrifice, you'll also actively begin creating situations that require them.

Here's a simple analogy: When you go to the gym, you add weights to the machines so that your muscles strain and you feel the burn. If you don't add enough weights and the training is easy, you feel that you haven't done the required exercise, that you've wasted your time, which, in the case of strength training, is perfectly reasonable. But there is no scientific evidence of any correlation between your emotional and physical strain and the realness or sustainability of your success.

In 1908, Robert M. Yerkes and John Dillingham Dodson conducted research on mice and concluded that moderate stress increases performance (of mice).[15] Consequently, Yerkes-Dodson law became the bible for hustlers and proponents of "moderate stress" for performance enhancement. One of the more peculiar ideas that took flight as a consequence of the moderate stress theory is the idea of "active procrastination." The idea is simple: If you want to perform at your maximum, push off a task at hand to the last limit, allowing yourself just enough time to perform the task. Moderate stress that arises from such procrastination will make you more productive.

A lot of people subscribe to this theory. And if you, too, choose to believe this theory, you will not only see in it proof of your beliefs, but you will create circumstances where you become living proof of the theory that you believe in.

And so, let me give you an alternative viewpoint, in case you would like to challenge the myth of hustling and find freedom from the "success equals hard work" paradigm.

Alfie Kohn, an educator and author of multiple books, said it perfectly:[16]

> The Yerkes-Dodson law, which has been floating around psychology for more than a century, holds that there is an ideal level of arousal for performing a given task. If the task is complex, there's often an inverted-U relationship, meaning that a medium level is better than either too little or too much. Most of us tend to fare best when a task is neither so simple as to be boring nor so hard as to produce anxiety. Of course, there are different ways that a task can be experienced as "hard." But the key point is that this fact about arousal (physiological activation) doesn't allow us to conclude that stress—something quite different, which typically connotes distress—is valuable at any level.

The myth of hustling is prevalent and has a lot of proponents. It is deeply rooted in our consciousness that we get almost outraged if anyone suggests otherwise. But let us look at how it grew such deep roots, and it might be easier to undo the damage from there.

Reflection Points

Today you are going to elaborate on the exercise from the last chapter, but you will do it with a twist.

Write a short essay—it can be just a few sentences or a few paragraphs—"Why are you *not* (sufficiently) successful?" I'm sure there's room for more success in your life, right?

Now reread what you have written and pay attention to generalisations. For example, "I don't have a lucrative profession," or "I cannot grow in my current job," or "I am too lazy, and I don't work enough." Write out such generalisations—these are your current (limiting) beliefs about success.

Ask yourself:

- Are these statements true?
- Can you see evidence to the contrary?
- Are there people who defy such ideas?

Forming new supportive beliefs will take time. Meanwhile, just notice your unsupportive thoughts. You can also say, "Cancel-cancel!" every time you think this way.

"SURFING" AS AN
Antidote
TO HUSTLING

*The difference between successful
people and really successful people
is that really successful people say
"no" to almost everything.*

— WARREN BUFFETT[17]

Imagine how your life would have evolved if, from an early age, you were told to put more effort into areas where you did well, rather than where you struggled?

As a perfect little Hermione for most of my life, I got a nationally famous "golden medal" for my academic excellence from the president of Estonia. But even that wasn't enough for the system.

When my mum went to school to meet with my teachers, one teacher said: "Kristina is doing well and her grades are excellent (dah!), but she's been slipping a bit with spelling and grammar in Russian. She needs to put more effort into Russian going forward."

There I was for years, putting all my efforts into a subject I had no passion for, a subject I was the "weakest" at, while my true passion, physics, went down the drain. I simply had no time to study what I was already good at.

But what if my teacher had told my mom, "Kristina is doing well, and her grades are good. And she is especially good with physics and mathematics, and she seems to really enjoy the sciences. Why don't you encourage her to put more effort into that area and see how she can learn it more deeply?"

How would your life look if you put most of your effort into subjects that you loved the most, that you enjoyed doing, and that you were naturally good at? How would you understand success then? Would you still equate it to blood, sweat, and tears? Or maybe it could be something that comes easily, even naturally?

I certainly do not want to say that we never need to put in any effort or do the hard work. Indeed, we do—I didn't get my golden medal from dancing and playing around. I had my share of sleepless nights and frustrating studying.

Yet hustling cannot be your default regime. It is unsustainable. What is the alternative, you may ask?

Let me introduce you to the concept of *flow* versus *resistance*. At any given time, you can be in one of the two states: you can be in a state of flow or in a state of resistance. Rest is flow: you don't apply any effort to rest your body and mind. Hustling is a state of resistance: you need to apply effort to hustle—it's like swimming upstream, or it is not hustling.

Naturally, rest is not the only state of flow, and hustling is not the only state of resistance. If you master a skill, which will be initially achieved through some resistance (applied effort), you can later perform that skill in a state of flow (no effort). For example, if you've been riding a bike since childhood, you can ride it without any resistance in a state of flow, even if the first few times you had to go through a lot of resistance battling with gravity and learning to balance.

In Western society, the default regime for success and achievement is hustling, and I was introduced to this concept early on in my career. In my first job in the Estonian government, I had a wonderfully lovely colleague, who always said "busy-busy" whenever she was asked how she was doing. A few years later, I moved to New York and learned the concept of "24/7." It took me a while to understand it in the context of "I'm busy 24/7," because it didn't make sense biologically.

You might ask: "How do you achieve anything if you don't hustle?" The answer, naturally, is by doing the exact opposite of hustling—by creating a state of flow.

Flow is a state that has been fairly well researched and dissected, yet it is a little hard to grasp, because it feels like it is out of our control. Our logic understands hustling, effort, hard work, hours, and sweat put into a job—it can be created and regulated with a simple calendar or a planner. But flow is a state that needs to be created, induced, and cannot be simply switched on with a clear ritual.

According to Steven Kotler,[18] one of the world's leading experts on optimising performance, empirical evidence shows that people are five times more productive when they operate in a state of flow. And so my alternative to hustling is *surfing*. You must have seen surfers gliding on the ocean before: little dots bobbing on the surface of the water, waiting for their wave to come. Once the wave comes, they get up on their surfboard and ride it to the shore with speed, efficiency, and excitement. This way of working is a lot more effective than hustling. Riding the waves of our own motivation and creativity will reap more results than hardcore working to the point of burnout.

Think of it this way—since you are five times more productive when you work in a state of flow, you could get done all the work you would have done Monday to Friday in just one working day.[19]

Flow is a creative state. *Hustling* is a state in which you maintain the status quo. Now the important nuance is this: surfing is not better than hustling, and hustling is not better than surfing. You need both (at times) to reach success, but you cannot make one of those states your default regime and avoid the other. In fact, ideally, if you were to choose one, choose surfing and hire a team to do the hustling. Why? Because hustling has a glass ceiling to it, and surfing is limitless.

As you can see, equating success to hustling, hard work, sweat and blood, hours put into a job, and sacrifice put on the altar of your success is a slippery slope. Not only because it will burn you out and take you off your path to your own unique brand of happiness, but because it is simply not true or realistic.

We do our best to do the right thing, adopting the myth of hustling and equating success to overcoming hardship and resistance. But what if that resistance you feel is your heart and intuition giving you signals that you are going full speed ahead . . . in the wrong direction?

Only when we allow ourselves to create in flow, embrace our weaknesses and work on our strengths, trust ourselves and respect our own truths, only then do we see the glimpse of the actual right direction.

Reflection Points

Your exercise today is called "Finding Your Superpowers." Make a list of your superpowers. List at least 10. These can be your skills, character traits, or things that you are really good at, like being supportive or finding humour in difficult situations.

Send e-mails to at least 10 people among your friends, family, and colleagues and ask them to tell you your three superpowers.

Wait for the answers, and next to your own list of 10 superpowers, write down what superpowers other people see in you. Compare the two lists:

- Which superpowers does the world see in you, which you are also aware of?

- Which superpowers do you think you have, but you have not shown them to the world yet?

- Which superpowers you did you not realise you had, but your friends, colleagues, and family can see them in you?

PART II

FINDING YOUR OWN

Truth

THE RED
Pill

*It is always a silly thing to give advice,
but to give good advice is absolutely fatal.*

— OSCAR WILDE[1]

Are you ready for the truth?

More importantly, are you ready to be honest with yourself? Are you ready to *honour* your truth, and stand up for it, even if it hurts? Now is the moment for me to give you a disclaimer, a warning.

You haven't gotten too far, so you can still turn back and forget everything you have read so far. You can keep your current life and your present image of yourself. You can go on as you have done before.

Don't continue reading a line more of this book if you are not ready for a big transformation—because you will never be able to *unread* it.

This is the moment to choose between the red pill and the blue pill. Reading the rest of the book? That will be you choosing the red pill. Putting it down—you are going with the blue.

You should know that I am not going to tell you the truth you are seeking. It won't come from me. Your truth is *your* truth, and my truth is *mine*. All I can do is to help you open up to yourself, find courage to take a flashlight and go into the basement of your beautiful building with a perfect facade, and shine the light into the darkest corners of the most forgotten nooks and crannies. It is there that you will find your dragons, which have been hiding in the dark, ignored and obliviated.[2]

I will help you find courage to look those dragons in the eye. I will support you in finding fortitude in your heart so you can be at peace with its abode in your beautiful and "perfect" house.

You can easily live alongside my truths or anyone else's truths without giving them too much attention, no matter how much they may contradict your own paradigms, beliefs, or values. But you will not be able to close your eyes and ignore your own red pill once you find it in your palm. And even if you choose not to swallow it, your life will not go back to what it was before.

I like to compare it to a hobbit's journey: you are now on your doorstep as Bilbo Baggins.[3] Once you set your foot on the path, you are on your own Hero's Journey. You have to walk the path, through mountains and forests, into the darkest cave. You have to find that dragon and face it. And if you live, you'll come out on the other side as a brand-new being.

Once you start walking, there's no going back. You see, authenticity is not a switch—you cannot flick it on and off at will. It is like a skydive. Once you step out of the plane door and pull the cord, your parachute opens and there is no way back—you cannot pack it back up into your bag mid-air and retrace your fall back up to the plane.

Sometimes, I look back at my life in my blissful 20s and 30s, and some parts of me want to go back to that perfectly easy and carefree time (or so it seems to me from the now). I wish I could wind back the clock, undo all the changes and transformation, unfeel all the pain that led to that transformation, screw up my eyes, and be blissfully happy in my previous life. Yes, sometimes my desire is to go back to a time when I was blissfully ignorant to my own depth, my own truth.

But I have taken my red pill, and there is no return for me.

I had spent 17 years of my life in Asia, but I was born and raised in Europe, and I felt keenly European during my life in the East. I dreamed of going back, of how beautiful it would be to live a simple European life—enjoy history and nature, little local shops and cafés, endless opportunities to experience art, music, and culture.

But my home and my whole life were in Asia. And so I created a little European oasis in the heart of my new home. I bought art, books, and musical instruments; I arranged European meals for my family; and I made sure that my children learned their mother tongue, Estonian.

I lived in this European doll house in the heart of Asia— until we finally summoned up the courage to move back to Europe, as a family. I had been dreaming about this move for so many long years, and finally, it was happening.

It wasn't a simple move. We had unexpected and frustrating hurdles along the way, but after a lot of waiting and fretting, I was finally on the plane about to land on European soil, bringing my family over to settle back into my own childhood hometown.

I vividly remember sitting on the plane near the window and looking at the land approaching. Suddenly, I felt fear, I felt uncertain, I wished that we wouldn't land so quickly—I wasn't ready! I wasn't ready to become a European once again. I suddenly felt so completely and totally Asian—the way I thought and felt about the world, my mentality, my habits, my way of life were shaped by the 17 years I had lived there, in a big family, accepted and integrated as Asia's own child.

In those 17 years away, so many things had changed. Estonia had changed, Tallinn had changed, my friends and family had changed—no doubt about that. But most importantly—I had changed. I was a new Kristina, landing in my imaginary world from the past. And my new life in the old world would never be the same.

There is now no way I can go back to my cosy old life, my old life as a married woman, my old life as a mom of young kids, my old life full of blue pills. No matter how romantically nostalgic my memories may be of that time in my life, the new me would not fit with my old life.

In fact, I think I would probably grab a sledgehammer and smash that old reality in a blink of an eye and return back to where I am right now: reinventing my life from a blank page, reinventing it by my own rules, following my own heart, standing up for my own truths.

So, are you ready for the red pill? Then, *let's go*!

Reflection Points

This exercise may seem a little uncomfortable. But these are important questions, which I want you to ask yourself before we move on:

- What are you most afraid of about reading this book?
- What are you afraid to discover or realise?
- Are you willing to change if you do not know who you are changing into?

You can write down your answers in the journal. Writing will help you to be more clear about your thoughts.

Buzzwords
COME WITH
BAGGAGE

A new idea is hatched; it begins to spread; it catches on; it inspires a flurry of books and articles, conferences and seminars. And then it fades away. In the last couple of decades, this cycle has played out many times in our field. Yet no matter how many iterations we witness, it can be hard to recognize that the pattern applies to whatever idea is currently stirring up excitement —or to understand the limits of that idea.

— ALFIE KOHN[4]

Although my intention is to support you in redefining and rediscovering your true self, this entire book is essentially about authenticity. Authenticity will become your trusty passport on the path back to yourself. It's pretty much all you need.

People often compliment me for being authentic, "really authentic," as if there is an option to be more or less authentic, absolutely or not-quite-so authentic. As I said in the opening of this book, authenticity is binary; it is not a scale. You cannot be 95 percent authentic. There is no second-degree of authenticity.

Before I go on with my story of finding the path back to myself, I'd like to make a little stop here and talk about some of the most important concepts we are going to be discussing in the rest of this book.

Every generation has its own language with its big, fashionable ideas and new(-ish) concepts, which seem to fascinate pretty much everyone at a particular time. As time goes by, our thoughts evolve, new ideas and concepts take over, and new language emerges.

Let's take personal growth as an example.

The concept of improving oneself is not new. As soon as humans learned abstract thinking, as soon as first philosophers, theologians, and storytellers emerged, the idea of improving oneself by certain practises, thoughts, or actions started evolving. It wasn't called "personal growth," or "self-help," or "transformational teachings," of course, but you will find traces of personal growth in writings throughout the whole of human history, from the stoics of ancient times, such as Seneca and Marcus Aurelius, to the forefathers of the contemporary personal growth industry, such as Napoleon Hill and Wallace D. Wattles.

Humans have always been obsessed with becoming better. Some of the most notable classical novels of the past are, in essence, about the evolution of a human being. One of my favourite authors, Russian novelist Fyodor Dostoevsky, considered himself a philosopher. I've learned and experienced more personal growth from his novels than from many of the most conventional teachers in the industry. Another favourite of mine, Jane Austen— through all her jest and sarcasm—was actually telling the story of how to be a better person.

My point is this: we have been thinking of how to improve ourselves for as long as we have been thinking.

And every generation has ideas and theories they are fascinated with. In Austen's time, it was about propriety and honour. In the trying times of the two world wars, it was about altruism and human dignity. In my Soviet childhood, being a better person meant sacrificing your personal wants to grand ideas and the greater good of society. When I was a student, we were fascinated by motivational speakers who gave us a kick on the butt to do more with our lives. That was the time of "unleashing the power within,"[5] "You can do it!" and "If not now, when?"

Later, the world became obsessed with the "law of attraction." Meditation and mindfulness became mainstream. And now you can talk about *awakening* to business people, who are quite comfortable with the idea of selling their Ferraris[6] and going away for a long vipassana retreat in a remote ashram.[7]

With the evolution of theories and ideas, our language evolves as well. We pick up words that are part of the latest thought evolution and give them an expanded, hefty meaning, which is often beyond the original definition of the word.

Take hustling, for example, a concept I was talking about previously. I used this word in its new, expanded, hefty definition of energetic perseverance, busy action, and "striving headstrong and voraciously toward a goal." It is quite far from the original definition of the word *hustle* that had a little tinge of underworld and illegality.

Or better yet, let's talk about meditation. I bet you pictured a person sitting cross-legged with closed eyes, possibly with dimmed lights, burning essences, cosy cushions, and quite possibly this picture could be expanded further to a peaceful mountain landscape with chimes ringing softly in the distance. Now, if you came upon this word in one of Jane Austen's novels, you would have to draw a different picture—a young woman with a handwritten letter in her hand, gazing into the distance and meditating about the meaning of the words she had just read.

The point I'm driving at is simple, but it alone might change your life completely. As much as we are used to shortcuts and simplifications, it will benefit you greatly if you learn to look beyond the buzz and notice the essence of things.

You will come across several buzzwords in this book. I would like to suggest that you read the next lines looking beyond the familiar words. The moment you see a buzzword, try to stop yourself from drawing a hefty and complete picture, which pops up as soon as you hear the word. Instead, blank out the buzz, go further, and tap into the essence of what I am describing.

Did you know that children who are bilingual by birth (more than half of the world population, by some estimates) have an interesting advantage compared to their monolingual peers? They have greater symbolic flexibility, which means that they understand that objects have different labels in different languages, and they can more easily separate form and meaning.[8] And that, in turn, gives bilingual kids incredible advantages from metalinguistic abilities to advantages in cognitive functioning,[9] reduced bias in decision-making,[10] understanding abstract concepts, and even better focusing abilities.[11]

You will benefit greatly in life if you learn to detach yourself from the hefty baggage that words inevitably come with, especially popular words, and see beyond the buzz into the essence of the phenomena. Just like bilingual kids, you improve your brain's functioning, you will discover new facets of the old and familiar things, understand people better, and be more tolerant and empathetic.

Reflection Points

Today, I want to suggest a simple exercise to you in which we will look into the essence of words behind their facade.

Pick one buzzword for this exercise—it can be *awareness, mindfulness, the law of attraction, perfectionism, hustling, awakening, happiness,* or anything you like. Whichever buzzword (or phrase) you pick for this exercise, it has to be a generally understood concept.

Your homework is to ask a few people to explain your selected concept to you. Ask at least three or more people how they understand the word that you've picked. And then notice what kind of baggage people are giving to otherwise familiar words. You may be surprised how different each perspective of the same word is.

An important rule: do not explain the concept to your interviewees; just try to understand the meaning that they give, and notice the difference between their answers. This exercise is better done in writing, so if you have patience, do the exercise by e-mail.

Authenticity IS INTERNAL

So we arrive at "authenticity," which has to do with our true self, our individual existence, not as we might present it to others, but as it "really is," apart from any roles we play.

— RICHARD HANDLER[12]

I was once speaking at an event about expanding influence, and my particular topic was, you guessed it, authenticity. Don't you find it a little ironic? I was to speak about authenticity as a means to expand one's influence in the world.

The problem here is that influence and authenticity are two forces with different directions. If we draw a simple analogy from mechanical physics, it is like pushing a balloon under water: the water pushes the balloon up while your hand is trying to push it down.

Influence is a vector, a force with outward direction. You exert your influence toward someone. Your actions, or words, make a change in another human being, and they may change their views, their thoughts, or their behaviour. You are the source of that force, and someone else is the object being changed by the force.

Authenticity is not a vector; it is a force that has no outward direction. Authenticity is your relationship with yourself. There is only you and no external object, no one but you to exert the force toward.

The moment you try to use authenticity as a means of influence, you are giving it a direction outward.

Consequently, authenticity loses its inherent quality of being your relationship with yourself, an internal process, a force with no outward direction. The moment you use authenticity to influence the world, it stops being authenticity and becomes something else entirely: a weapon, a crown, a costume—something to impress others.

And that is why I find it amusing when people compliment me about my authenticity. They may perceive me being authentic, but that has more to do with how they feel, not how I feel. Thus, their judgement has nothing to do with me being authentic or inauthentic. Since authenticity is an internal process, only I can know if I am being authentic or if I am using tricks to make people think or feel in a certain way. I am the only judge of my own authenticity.

Authenticity is an epitome of a buzzword. It has a rather narrow, traditional meaning, but it has acquired hefty baggage over the past few years. Yet there is very little study on authenticity and virtually no scientific research on the topic.[13] Consequently, it is greatly misunderstood, and the most concerning misunderstanding about authenticity is linking it to the outside world:

Can you **appear** to be authentic?

Can you **show** or display your authenticity?

Can you **influence** your relationships with others through authenticity?

Can you **use** authenticity to create trust? Or drive a message?

And the most feared question:

Can you be **rejected** because of your authenticity?

Yes, and no.

Authenticity is internal, remember. It is the resulting state of healing your most important relationship: your relationship with yourself, not anyone else. It's the core essence of this simple phenomenon.

So when it comes to being authentic, how the outside world perceives you or reacts to you is irrelevant.

In addition, contrary to popular belief, your self-perception isn't defined by the outside world either. It is an illusion—the way you react to the outside world is ultimately defined by your self-perception.

Here's a simple example to illustrate this profound idea:

When you hear criticism about yourself or your actions, your reaction to the critical feedback depends on how much you believe it to be true. You are more likely to be hurt by the criticism that you agree with on some level.

If you are emotional and someone throws an "Oh, don't be so dramatic!" at you, you will likely feel hurt. But if someone criticises you for something you don't identify with at all, you are most likely going to feel nothing about such criticism. In simple words, you would not be upset if I said that green hair doesn't look good on you, unless your hair was really green.

It is my hope that this book supports you as you sever the connection between your self-perception and the outside world in one fell swoop.

And this idea may seem intimidating at first, because we're afraid that if we sever this connection, our relationships will change. We are afraid of rejection: "If I show who I really am, people will not like me." But as we established, it is an illusion to think that the outside world can change your relationship with yourself.

So work on your relationship with yourself. Once you have this one sorted, all your other relationships will fall into place.

Reflection Points

Today's exercise is going to be light and easy. Ponder these questions:

- How do you define authenticity?
- What does authenticity feel like to you?
- How do you know when you are being authentic?
- What makes you authentic?

You can write down your answers in your journal.

Vulnerability
& CROCODILE TEARS

Oversharing? Not vulnerability; I call it floodlighting. . . .
A lot of times we share too much information
as a way to protect us from vulnerability.

— BRENÉ BROWN[14]

Let's examine another hugely fashionable buzzword: *vulnerability*.

And here, once again, I ask you to stop, take a deep breath, and pretend that you have never heard this word before. What if you were to cast away its hefty baggage and try to see behind the ornate facade into the essence of the concept?

Vulnerability is a loaded word. Its baggage is not just heavy; it is extremely emotionally charged. Whenever this word pops up, a wide range of emotions surface: from shame, fear, and reluctance to passionate generalisations and glorification.

Now, just to be clear, I'm not against people being more vulnerable. I salute vulnerability; I recognise it as a courageous act; and I am fully conscious and aware that being vulnerable is a prerequisite for building strong, meaningful connections. I am a supporter of vulnerability.

But what I do rebel against is "vulnerability tyranny," which seems to be plaguing contemporary society.

Even Brené Brown, the queen of vulnerability, the most avid vulnerability advocate of all time, a scientist who has researched the phenomenon deeply, came up with a curious (contradictory) idea recently—that "vulnerability without boundaries is not vulnerability."[15]

Vulnerability is like chocolate—too much of a good thing can become bad. Too much vulnerability isn't vulnerability—rather, it's tyranny, an unhealthy unloading of emotion.

When it comes to vulnerability, it is a beautiful skill— in the right place and at the right time. And like with anything else in life, there may be too little of it, or too much of it. And, most notably, not everything that looks like vulnerability is actually the real thing.

Here's what vulnerability is *not*:

- It is not about sharing your deepest, darkest, personal secrets in public.

- It is not about expressing intensely painful emotions in public.

- It is not about crying in public.

Rather, in her famous TED talk,[16] Brené Brown talks about vulnerability in the context of creating strong human connections:

> They [research subjects] didn't talk about vulnerability being comfortable, nor did they really talk about it being excruciating. . . . They just talked about it being necessary. They talked about the willingness to say, "I love you" first . . . the willingness to do something where there are no guarantees . . . the willingness to breathe through waiting for the doctor to call after your mammogram. They're willing to invest in a relationship that may or may not work out.

Vulnerability is "the willingness to do something where there are no guarantees." It is about being brave, but not just brave. It is the willingness to do something in the face of uncertainty.

So it seems vulnerability has two vital ingredients: courage *and* uncertainty.

Let me now give you two examples from my own experience, and I'd like you to be the judge of my vulnerability in each.

I love telling jokes. I love to laugh, especially at my mistakes or blunders. But I'm not very good at telling jokes, and if there is one profession that I cannot imagine ever doing, it's being a comedian. Nevertheless, I love telling jokes, and I often do, sometimes awkwardly, sometimes ill-timed, sometimes very well and to the point. I tell jokes from a stage to relax the tension of stage fright. I tell jokes at meetings to lighten up the atmosphere. I tell jokes to strangers to break the ice. But the last time I remember telling an awkward joke, it was met with icy silence, and I felt very uncomfortable.

On the other hand, as a speaker with some years of experience, I have a few personal stories, which tend to hit nerves. People relate to them, and they often feel emotional when I relay them. I've told some of my stories several times, I've polished them, I've tried them out. I know how people react to them. And, at times, I still feel emotional while sharing those personal experiences. I may shed a public tear I would prefer to keep back, but I know exactly the reaction that my stories will evoke in my audience. In a way, these deeply private stories have become my means of influence because they help me achieve a certain reaction I need to get out of my audience.

Which of those two situations is more vulnerable for me?

Which truly has both ingredients: courage *and* uncertainty?

Is it possible that, in this case, joking around could be more vulnerable than crying on stage?

I think it's a slippery slope when we equate vulnerability to deep personal secrets, intense painful emotions, and tears. When we brush over what actually makes someone vulnerable—courage in the face of uncertainty—we lose the sense of the original meaning and end up associating it with overt honesty. I can tell you this much from my own personal experience: I have very reserved friends who are perfectly honest, authentic, and trustworthy. And I've met incredibly vulnerable people who were at the same time self-obsessed, narcissistic manipulators.

Vulnerability is important. And I celebrate the fact that vulnerability has been normalised, and in fact, its value is now universally accepted. But authenticity is more important, quite simply, because it must come first. First, your relationship with yourself—authenticity. And once this most important relationship is sorted, then comes your relationship with the outside world—aka vulnerability.

Hence, equating vulnerability with authenticity misses the mark. You can be vulnerable and, at the same time, be completely delusional, live in your made-up world, resort to immature coping strategies rather than deal with your painful emotions. So you can be vulnerable but stay inauthentic. I'll put it bluntly: you can vulnerably expose your messed-up inner psyche to the big, wide world and be no more honest with yourself.

On the other hand, you can be completely authentic, know yourself profoundly, face your dragons, stay true to yourself, and still choose not to be vulnerable in certain circumstances. You may choose not to open up to strangers or take your time before you feel at ease in a new company. You may choose not to take risks in unfamiliar circumstances. You may choose to be closed or even introverted to feel safe. Yet, such choices don't make you any less authentic or less true to yourself. In fact, you may choose to take your time because you are at peace with being introverted, cautious, modest, shy, whatever the reason why you don't want to be vulnerable.

In summary, there's a big difference between vulnerability and crocodile tears. Vulnerability without authenticity is the latter, and can become an instrument for influence, manipulation, and even tyranny.

Kids know this very well. They learn it at a very tender age and use the concept masterfully on their parents. In my family, we use the code words *crocodile tears* to figure out how to deal with drama. When my daughter Eve was younger and used to burst out in tears, I needed to know whether they were genuine and Eve needed proper adult consolation and support, or if she was just making a show to drive a point, because her vocabulary was still too limited to express the minor facets of her frustration. If it was the latter, she would whisper to me with a chuckle, "crocodile tears," and I knew that the situation was to be taken with lightness and humour.

My friends, children use tears and intense emotions to manipulate. You know this. *But adults do this too.* Even if they do it a little more elegantly, without throwing themselves down on the floor in the middle of the toy aisle in a store.

Reflection Points

Think of a recent situation when you were feeling vulnerable.

- What made the situation uncertain?
- Why did you choose to be courageous despite the uncertainty?
- How did you feel as result of your brave vulnerability?

As usual, you can write down your answers in the journal.

CALLING OUT THE
Critic

*Nothing I accept about myself
can be used against me to diminish me.*

— AUDRE LORDE[17]

When did I become too old to wear shorts in public?

I was puzzled to remember the day I looked at myself in the mirror and said: "No, you are too old for that!"

More importantly, why did I make such a verdict on myself? I don't want to wear shorts in public because I think it is inappropriate at my age. I'm not talking about wearing hot pants to the office, that would be mostly inappropriate at any age. Although, who am I to judge? To be honest, I'm wearing my classic Daisy Dukes right now at home because they are comfortable. Yet my Daisy Dukes plus a public place (not the office) are somehow inappropriate.

I'm worried that a hypothetical stranger might look at me and think: "She's a bit too old to wear shorts in public."

Wait a minute! The judgement I'm passing on myself is based on what a hypothetical stranger might think about me? Well, for a start, I don't even know if strangers *do* think about me. They probably don't. But even if they did and their opinion, somehow, did matter, it's impossible for strangers to accept or reject me. They will have their opinions regardless of my choices. We often make decisions when "thinking of others." But can we actually affect their feelings? Can we shift them one way or another? And more importantly, what makes something "okay" or "not okay"? When is that decision made?

A stranger's opinion is a little bit like a Schrödinger's Cat (the famous quantum physics thought experiment)—it's just as likely to be a rejection as it is not. As long as the cat is in the steel box, it might be both: equally dead and alive.

Our feelings and thoughts toward other people have more to do with us than with the people we are having feelings about. Our thoughts about other people are reflections of how we feel about ourselves.

You see, the world will treat you the way you will train it to treat you. It is a hard truth to swallow, it may be unpleasant to admit, but, in most cases, that is exactly what happens.

If we don't expect respect, we will very likely be insulted. If we don't expect justice, we will very likely be taken advantage of. If we don't expect love and acceptance, we are very likely going to be rejected.

It is a simple equation.

So who has the power to reject or accept you? You've guessed it: you. You are your first critic. And then you put on your own decision like a dress and go out into the world with it, getting exactly what you expect.

Just as when we wear costumes and different-style clothes to different occasions, and those costumes and clothes shape our personality in those circumstances. When you go to a serious business meeting, you wear something professional, and you feel a little more professional and ready for the meeting. When you go for a romantic date, you wear something hot, and it makes you feel more attractive. When you put on your sports outfit to go to the gym, you feel a little more fit and energised the moment you put on those clothes. We wear our opinions about ourselves, and they shape our personality just the same way that clothes do.

Thus, when I put on my shorts and go out feeling that I'm too old to wear them, my judgement of myself is like a veil over what I'm actually wearing.

On the flip slide, I may feel extra sexy and attractive wearing beautiful underwear, even if no one else can see it, just because of *how it feels*.

And so here's the most important point: the only person whose rejection you have to fear is your own. As long as you can accept yourself, the world has no choice but to accept you as well. And if it doesn't, you won't give a damn anyway.

Reflection Points

Are you ready for a fun experiment? I invite you to wear something unusual, something you don't normally wear. You can borrow clothes if you need to. It may be an immaculate professional suit, or a hard-core biker outfit, or a long, ladylike, flowing dress.

You can wear an unusual undergarment, maybe something sexy, or you can experiment with suspenders or accessories. It is a good idea to wear something that no one can see or know about.

Go out for a walk or meet with your friends, or even go to the office if it is appropriate. Notice how your new clothes make you feel.

- Do you feel uncomfortable? If so, why do you feel uncomfortable?
- Do you feel empowered? If so, what makes you feel different?
- Has anything changed in the way people treat you? If so, how did it change?

STARVING YOUR

Delusions

All of us are a little delusional. We live in a "reality" created in our own heads, and every day, wherever we go and whatever we do, we find evidence to prove our perception of reality is the "right" one.

Do you remember the exercise we did previously, when you had to notice different colours in your environment? You were mostly noticing the colour I had asked you to focus on, and it was harder to recall the colour that you did not think about in the process of examining your environment. This happens because your goal determines your perception: the reticular activating system dictates the way you perceive the world.

And I'm not talking about the law of attraction here—it is simple psychology and no magic.

I was once talking to a 25-year-old man at a friend's wedding in Russia. We were discussing longevity, and I was shocked to hear this young guy retort: "I'm not going to live to a hundred years. Nobody does! Look around—people are dying when they are seventy. Or they are so old and miserable: Who even wants to live to be old?"

I tried to bring up hard evidence—research, new data, scientific evidence, and examples from the Blue Zones[19]—but he looked at me as if I was completely out of my mind.

In this man's reality, nobody lived until 100 years old. And even if they did, in his reality, they were old, sick, and miserable. That was what he believed in, and he had sufficient evidence to prove himself right in his environment.

To this young guy's credit, I must admit that the average life expectancy in Russia at the time of our conversation was 72 years, so he was completely justified to stand firm on his viewpoint. But the trick is in opening your mind to *new* evidence.

Just like in our little experiment with colours, the moment you allow a suggestion, the moment you accept a hypothesis, you will suddenly start "stumbling" on the evidence to support your new hypothesis.

And this is the curious thing about the world: There is no absolute truth. Whatever you believe in, is true—for you.

So, you see, it's not an exaggeration to say that each of us is a little delusional. The question is, what kind of delusion do you choose to live in? And what do you believe to be "true" about yourself?

Dove, a world-famous personal care brand, once conducted a brilliant experiment with French women.[20] The selected women were asked to record their thoughts about themselves, their inner self-talk. Whenever they had a thought about themselves or how they looked, the women wrote it down in a diary.

What kind of thoughts do you think about yourself? When you wake up in the morning, go to the bathroom, and look into the mirror—what does your self-talk sound like?

In the Dove experiment, the women were asked to record their thoughts about themselves. Then their diaries were collected, and some of the most horrifying entries were used for the second part of the experiment. Two actresses were to act out in public, in a café, in a "friendly" chat. One of the actresses was to memorise the horrifying diary entries and recite them in public to her friend, the second actress, as if they were just having a natural conversation. So she would say: "Your legs are too short," or "Other women have charm; you have none."

But here's the twist. The women from the experiment were inconspicuously invited to sit in the same café and hear their own words recited to another woman. They were listening to their own self-talk as bystanders. Can you guess what their reactions were like?

The women were shocked to hear their own words thrown at another woman, because they were too strong, too hard, too unfair. One of them couldn't bear it and interrupted: "You cannot talk like this to your friend!"

Granted, the whole experiment was shot for a Dove brand awareness campaign, but it is such a brilliant and vivid example of how hard we are on ourselves. "You cannot talk like this to your friend!" Yet we talk to ourselves like this all the time. And no one is calling us out about it.

Your self-talk is often so harsh and unkind that you would never talk like that to another person. And then your brain picks up those unkind thoughts and words, your judgement and criticism, and gets to work. Your goal defines your perception, and you start seeing proof of your unkindness toward yourself, and then, your hard and critical judgement of yourself becomes a "reality" in your head. No wonder rejecting yourself becomes so easy!

I'm not talking about absolute rejection or giving up on yourself. I'm talking about the little stabs you give yourself for not being better, for not being perfect, for not being good enough. Oh, well—you know how many reasons there are to be hard on yourself!

Yet your "reality" is just an illusion, a delusion, because it is created by you in the first place. And the nature of self-deception is that you are usually not aware of being deceived. If you were aware of your delusion, it would become a point of view, a paradigm, a set of rules you consciously created for yourself. But without the awareness, whatever goes through your head is feeding the delusion.

And if you think you are too clever, too experienced, too sharp to be deceived, here's another interesting concept: a powerful mind can create a bulletproof illusion. We like to be right, and our brain is hard at work to prove us right, no matter the essence of what we want to be right about. Your brain's task, by default, is to make you think that you are right. So, naturally, the more powerful the brain, the stronger the delusion.

So how do you wake up from a powerful, self-deprecating delusion? The answer is simple: it starts with awareness. And this is exactly what we are going to be talking about in the next section.

Reflection Points

Let's do the Dove experiment together. I want you to write down your self-talk throughout the day.

I suggest you start tomorrow, first thing in the morning. Notice what you think or say in your head about yourself. A good place to start is your bathroom, when you look in the mirror and pick up a toothbrush. Notice what is going on in your head.

And write down your thoughts in your diary (that you'll carry with you) throughout the day, or you might forget them. Write down the exact words that you are using, even if they are not nice. (No one but you will be reading this later.)

In the evening, I'd like you to take some time and go through what you have written down. Imagine that you are saying these things to someone that you love: your friend, parent, child. If you have the courage, you can ask a friend to listen while you read out this self-talk.

Finally, ask yourself, how does it make you feel to talk like this to other people? And why do you talk like this to yourself?

PART III

SWITCHING
OFF
Autopilot

Escaping
THE RUT

*It is a hard thing to leave any deeply
routined life, even if you hate it.*

— JOHN STEINBECK[1]

My path to personal growth was winding and serendipitous. It wasn't a conscious choice. Rather, my life took me there.

I didn't resist because it felt right to me. On the other hand, my life could have taken me in any direction— sports, the big corporate world, politics, anything. If my husband, my job, or my people were anything else but personal growth and transformation junkies, I could have ended up doing something else entirely.

But my life took a turn toward personal growth, and I let the currents take me as far as they would. I might have not resisted the process, but neither was I very conscious about it.

It was about 12 years ago when I ended up at a goal-setting training workshop. To be honest, I was just tagging along with Vishen (my husband at the time) because his work required him to attend such events and meet the teachers. We spent three days redefining our life in every possible area down to the most minute detail. We reevaluated our beliefs, our daily practises, and our expectations in every area of life, from the obvious career and family stuff to the less common life categories, such as our character, emotional life, and quality of living. And in each of those areas, we set a bunch of goals to achieve.

By the evening of day three, I had hundreds of important goals lined up to be conquered. But that was not the end of the process. We spent the fourth day analysing and prioritising our goals.

The idea was to pick one goal to conquer them all, one goal that is the most important because it supports most of the other goals. We were to pick the goal that would create the biggest impact and be the most powerful thrust toward our ideal life. And then, we were to dedicate the next 30 days to this one goal.

Can you guess what my one mega-goal to rule them all was?

I decided to develop a skill that would be the most beneficial to me on my path to my perfect life.

And that new skill? *Awareness.*

I spent the next 30 days training myself to become more aware, living with an enhanced level of consciousness and purpose, with an aversion to autopilot.

For 30 days, I set up all kinds of reminders for myself to practise. I anchored the idea to everyday activities—brushing my teeth, walking up the stairs, sitting down to a meal. And, eventually, I remembered my task so well that I could pause for a second at any time during the day and tell myself: "Practise awareness—make the next decision with awareness."

Not surprisingly, my biggest discovery was how many decisions I'd been taking in my life robotically, without thinking, without even considering the bigger picture. I have never struggled with bad habits per se. I've picked up and dropped a few over the course of my life, but I never had extreme ones ruining my life. My life wasn't a mess; I didn't suffer from an unhealthy lifestyle, toxic relationships, drudgery, or routine. And yet my life was run by habits, subconscious patterns, and repetitive scenarios. I was functioning on autopilot.

Are you aware of the habits that are running your life? If you want to make a profound lasting change and turn your life around, you have to start at the root—you have to escape the rut of your habits and undo the programmes that have been running your life. And it starts with awareness.

Reflection Points

I want to share my favourite exercise with you. We are going to practise awareness. Do this exercise for at least 30 days. This is how it goes.

Set 5–10 reminders on your phone throughout the day. Every time the alarm rings, it is a reminder for you to practise awareness. Stop for a moment and notice what is going on.

- What are you doing at this very moment?
- Is it your conscious choice or are you acting on autopilot?
- What are the long-term consequences of whatever you are doing at this particular moment?

The main goal of this exercise is to stop living on autopilot and bring awareness into your day-to-day life. I am not asking you to change anything about your life. All I want is for you to notice what is going on.

THE POWER OF
Habits

Ill habits gather by unseen degrees,
as brooks make rivers, rivers run to seas.

— OVID[2]

Let's do a little experiment. The following chart represents weeks in a human's lifetime, assuming you are going to live to 100. I really love this chart because it is a powerful reminder of the finality of our most important resource: time.

Prevalence of big decisions in a lifetime

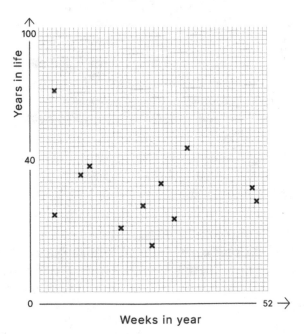

If you were to colour the squares on this chart, when you took big, life-changing, important, defining decisions, such as starting university, committing to your life partner, starting a business or a career, buying a house, or having children, you would probably colour about a dozen squares.

Now ask yourself, how much did these decisions shape your life? You might be tempted to say that they were the cornerstones of your life, the framework, the pillars supporting your life's structure. But here's the next question for you.

Can you think of some other people who made decisions similar to yours? Grew up in a town like yours, got the same kind of education, had a similar job to yours, and lived in your city with exactly the same kind of family setup as yours? How similar or dissimilar is their life to yours?

When I was a young mum, I used to get invariably frustrated when people tried to introduce me to "other mums like yourself." When I moved to Malaysia, I would be puzzled when people tried to introduce me to someone else from Estonia or thereabouts. I found such markers rather weak predictors of strength or closeness of a possible friendship, and they were lacking in evidence that such introductions were even worth my time.

In fact, I did end up with one lifelong friend from such introductions—a young mother from Estonia who used to live in Malaysia. But she was rather the proof of how weak such arguments were, because in years of introductions, she was the only real friend that I acquired.

My point is, even if we make similar big decisions in life, we don't end up living similar lives. That's why it was so hard for me to find common ground with people who happened to have made a few decisions in their lives in line with my own.

The "decorations" may often be similar. But the essence of our life is comprised of something entirely different.

I believe that in spite of any big defining decisions, our quality of life consists of daily, mundane, small choices, thoughts, and feelings. Yes, big decisions or unexpected life-changing events can throw you off balance for a while, but you will come back to your default state sooner or later, and your life will continue to be formed by your small daily choices. For example:

- What do you eat for breakfast? Or, better yet, what do you decide to do when you are hungry in the middle of the day: snack, have a meal, eat a chocolate?

- How do you move around during the day? Do you take elevators and escalators, or do you walk up the stairs? Do you drive in your car, take a bus, or would you rather walk if it is not too far?

- How do you interact with people? When you are confronted or contradicted? When you are wronged or misjudged? How do you react? What do you say?

- How do you relax after work? How do you interact with your family? How do you spend your weekends?

- How do you react to making a mistake, to rejection, to failure? What is your self-talk? What conclusions do you draw? Do you get back in the saddle? How fast?

Let's do another experiment. How many such small decisions do you take during the day? Can you guess a number without peeking into the next paragraph?

Researchers cannot agree on the exact number, but it is somewhere between 70 and 35,000 decisions per day.[3]

So, here you have a dozen important defining decisions in your life versus thousands of small and seemingly insignificant daily decisions.

But how insignificant are such decisions *really*?

First, we form our habits. Then, our habits form us. Our daily actions shape themselves into habits, then our habits shape themselves into our character, and our character shapes our entire life.

And the fact that habits shape our life isn't even the real problem. The more pressing issue is that those habits run (us) on *autopilot*. Often, we are not even aware of them to begin with.

Have you ever seen yourself on a video, only to realise that you keep fixing your hair without any obvious need, or that you rub your nose when you're thinking? Maybe you've heard yourself speak on an audio recording and realised that you use filler words, or suffuse thinking pauses with unintelligible sounds?

Another example of living on autopilot is doing things without realising *how* you did them. Have you ever left home without a clear memory of locking the door? Or, maybe, you had started to make tea and then found it hours later waiting for you on a countertop? Or maybe you began to drive home, only to realise halfway there that you were driving to your old address.

That's another interesting concept: your habits shape your life whether you are aware of them or not. In fact, such habits, the ones that run on autopilot without your awareness, have even more power over you. A simple example would be our thought patterns. Optimists and pessimists (and realists, if you like) have clearly very different thought patterns and, consequently, very different life experiences.[4]

So, let me ask you again: Which of your decisions have shaped your life the most?

When I did my 30-day awareness experiment, I found a lot of interesting habits which, I realised, didn't serve me anymore. They didn't ruin my life per se, but I could easily replace them with habits that were more fulfilling.

For example, I realised that mindless watching of movies and playing my piano were equally relaxing to me. I realised that eating something sweet while I was hungry did not quench my hunger, but rather made me feel worse. I realised how much time I was wasting driving and how I could be driven and use that commute time more productively. I realised that I enjoyed puzzles and learning languages, but that I had not done any such stimulating activities since I was in school.

As a result of my 30-day experiment, in addition to acquiring the most useful habit of doing things with awareness, I picked up some new hobbies: learning languages for fun, playing the harp, and doing art. My life, suddenly, became more colourful, and I felt a whole lot younger doing non-work-related creative tasks.

Some 10 years later, my life is new again. I have new hobbies, new habits, new routines. They are adjusted to my new life circumstances, but they do not happen blindly on autopilot anymore. I choose how I want to live every day.

A more recent example is this very book. It took an inexcusably long time to start my book. I was determined; I had a publisher; I knew what I was going to write about.

In fact, my students would keep telling me that I had to write a book. But with all of that, I was still stuck, and for several months, my new book baby consisted of page one, blank, open on my dashboard until I remembered that big projects are completed in small everyday steps. And so, I added a "book writing" slot to my calendar—each day, 30 minutes, for as long as it took to complete the book.

However, 30 days later, I had to admit that my initial genius arrangement needed a dramatic change. I was moving on, but slowly.

It is in moments like this where we need awareness once again: What is not working?

I realised it was the timing. What I needed was a vacuum of peace, and the only time when I could have peace was early morning, before everyone and everything were up and busy.

Nevertheless, I took the risk and slotted in my "book writing" at 8:00 A.M. Even though I thought that I was a night owl, I made this risky change in my schedule. And what did I discover? I might like to sleep late, and I might have more energy to do sports in the afternoon, but I absolutely loved writing early in the morning with my big cup of coffee, my daughter still peacefully asleep, and the morning sounds of a waking street outside the window.

That is when things really took off with good speed. It took one committed decision and a small daily habit to find the pattern that worked, and the most important ingredient, awareness, throughout the whole process. When we pick our routines and habits with awareness, we can start creating our life, rather than going with the flow passively to see where it takes us.

Reflection Points

I want to give you a different iteration of the awareness exercise from the previous chapter—another way to practise this fundamental skill.

Anchor the practise of awareness to your daily routines—brushing your teeth (my favourite), commuting, eating a meal, getting dressed. Break the pattern. Do these familiar daily tasks in a completely new way: brush your teeth with your nondominant hand, take a new route to work, take in the sight and smell of your food before you eat it, or take a moment to think where your food might have come from, or change the style of your clothes.

You can do these two iterations of the awareness exercise simultaneously—set up phone alarms and anchor the practise to your daily routines. Or you can try this second iteration for a few days and then get back to the first iteration from the previous chapter. Whichever version you choose, make sure that you practise awareness for 30 days.

 Don't
FORCE IT

Research makes clear that the best way to reach one's goal is not to resist temptations but to avoid temptations before they arrive; it further suggests that willpower is fragile and not to be relied on; and that the best self-regulators engage in willpower remarkably seldom.

— MICHAEL INZLICHT[5]

Imagine that one day you decide that you are going to take your health seriously—you woke up with a burning desire to live a healthy lifestyle. Often, what people do is hit the ground running: "From now on I'm doing everything right—I'll eat well; in fact, I'll cook at home, I'll exercise five times a week, I'll get a gym membership and buy good gym clothes (to give myself extra motivation), I'll go to bed earlier, I'll do a blood test and have my health checked," etc., etc.

And you take off with enthusiasm, and for a while, this passion makes you move in the right direction. Unfortunately, most of the time, such heel turns do not last long.

People lose motivation and interest toward the topic of their recent passion. The need for change is not as intense as it was in the beginning, and just the idea that one has done something to solve the problem, the proverbial first step, which is half of the journey, makes one feel accomplished and somewhat relieved.

At that point, the only thing you can do is start relying on your willpower:

- I can will myself to eat less for the rest of my life.

- I can will myself to do boring workouts every day.

- I can will myself to give up sugar/coffee/smoking.

- I can will myself to stop stressing and feeling anxious.

Does this sound familiar, my Good Boys and Good Girls?

Unfortunately, willpower doesn't work in the long run.[6] Willpower is a short-term strategy, so when you want consistent, sustainable change, you have to find a better strategy, something with less resistance.

Power of Incremental Changes

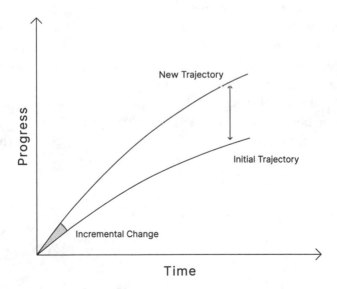

People often underestimate the power of small changes. We want it all and we want it right now! The bigger the pain, the more you are willing to sacrifice to change the situation, the more you are willing to invest. But heel turns are usually not sustainable in the long run. They may be, if you have a lot of iron willpower. But you will not enjoy life very much, because you will be in constant resistance.[7]

If you want sticky changes, they have to be incremental. When you adjust your course by just a few degrees, the shift in your life's trajectory, in the long run, will be enormous. And the longer you sustain that little change, the bigger its effect becomes. In financial investments, compounding is considered to be the way to generate huge returns.[8] Investing in your dream life is the same: small, incremental changes and compounding bring about the biggest and most sustainable change.

In our earlier example, rather than buying a gym membership and starting on a five-day training ritual, start walking more and taking stairs rather than elevators as the first easy habit, then add a physical activity that you really enjoy, then add a bit more, and a bit more—you get the idea: incremental, consistent changes.

Just as we discussed in the previous chapter, it's not your big, life-altering decisions that make the most significant difference in life; it is the small daily choices that matter the most.

Reflection Points

If you have been struggling with giving up a bad habit or creating a good new habit, take a moment of introspection. Ask yourself:

- Why are you struggling with this habit?
- Do you have many temptations that trigger your bad habit? How do you resist temptations? Do you often rely on willpower?
- What motivates you to develop the new good habit? Do you often rely on willpower?
- How does this struggle make you feel?
- Do you have relapses? And if you do, how does it make you feel?

The point of this exercise is not to judge yourself, but to pay attention to how the process of changing your habits makes you feel. So approach it with curiosity.

A BETTER
Fuel

Watch your thoughts, they become words;
watch your words, they become actions;
watch your actions, they become habits;
watch your habits, they become character;
watch your character, for it becomes your destiny.

— COLLOQUIAL WISDOM[9]

Here's the reason why awareness is such a powerful habit. When you combine incremental changes with awareness, you are able to find the most important ingredient for a lasting and sustainable shift in your life: intrinsic motivation.[10]

Psychologists say that the only mechanism that can sustain a change in your behaviour for a long time is motivation. You need to find strong motivation to make your desired change stick. Motivation has to be real and ongoing, not simply a violent and volatile, passionate outburst. Such motivation has to be strong enough to last, like a flickering flame, when you are in the middle of your deepest, darkest tunnel and you still don't see the light at the end of it. This motivation has to last when things get hard, when you lose faith in yourself, when you lose faith in the world and the people who are supposed to be on your side.

Once you find such strong motivation, you will not need iron will, unquenchable enthusiasm, and undying grit. You will naturally feel what you need to feel to keep going. Your grit and persistence will be fuelled by motivation, not willpower.

How do you find such strong motivation? Well, you need awareness in the process, but first, you need to take it one little step at a time. Heel turns require willpower because you cannot find one compelling, strong, over-arching motivation to do it all: eat healthy, cook at home, exercise daily, and go to sleep early. Yes, being healthy is a good motivation, but it is too broad, abstract, and vague to motivate you to a variety of vastly different efforts. In fact, the overarching goal, being healthy, is extrinsic in nature: a prize for living a good life.

It is when you break up your big shift into incremental changes that you are able to find intrinsic motivation in each of your smaller actions. Your motivation for cooking at home and exercising daily will not be the same. The driving force for you to perform those unfamiliar tasks will not be the same. The driving force for what makes cooking at home enjoyable will not be the same as what will make exercising daily fun.

But above all, you have to believe the colloquial wisdom that opened this chapter.

Notice the self-talk that comes with your new desired change (awareness required, again), because that is what will define your chances to find intrinsic motivation in all your new behaviours, and ultimately, this is what will determine your success.

You might have realised when you read the first part of this book that I do not like "hard work," or rather, I don't believe in it. That is not to say that I have never worked hard.

A lot of people say that writing a book is hard, running a business is hard, raising children is hard, combining work with family is hard.

Well, let's take book-writing for instance. I do not believe that it is hard. Does it require patience and persistence? Definitely! Is it sometimes confusing, and do I have to overcome challenging moments occasionally? Absolutely! And writer's block is a real thing, for sure. And in addition to all that, writing a book is also interesting, exciting, calming, clarity-inducing, inspiring, and many more amazing things. But it is not hard because, if it were, I wouldn't stick to it.

Do you see where I'm going here? For my new habit of book-writing to stick, I needed to find out what made the process desirable for me. But let's take it a notch deeper.

I have been speaking on stage since I was about 18 on a variety of different topics and with all kinds of messages. I've enjoyed speaking, but I never considered myself a professional speaker. I've always admired compelling, passionate speakers, and frankly, I often felt like an impostor.

I have to be candid with you—as a speaker, I am . . . okay. I know some tricks of the trade, even if I rarely use them. For instance, I am not incredibly animated or passionate on stage. My jokes are rather timid, and I am not always fully comfortable engaging the listeners. Nevertheless, I am lively and real, I can hold an audience, I have a talent for making people cry, I confess, and I have had people tell me that my speeches have changed their lives.

I've enjoyed speaking in public for years, and that kept me going back to the stage over and over again. But as a speaker, I matured much later. When I finally believed in the value that I had to offer, my message matured, and it gave me the fuel to finally *own* the stage, to believe that I earned the right to be on stage. My *message* became the motivation, not the thrill of public speaking itself.

The deeper your motivation, the more intrinsic it is to your actions, the easier it is to sustain the change that you are seeking to create in your life.

Reflection Points

This time, we are going to add a little twist to the awareness exercise (from the first chapter of Part III, "Escaping the Rut"), which I hope you are still practicing—30 days, as agreed.

Every time your phone alarm rings, I want you to pause, pay attention to the present moment, and ask yourself if what you are doing is your conscious decision, or if you are acting on autopilot.

And here's the twist: remove judgement. Just notice what you are doing. Ask yourself how it is affecting you, but do not make conclusions, such as "I have to stop doing this," or "I have to start doing that."

It is often our judgement of what we should or should not do that forces us to rely on willpower. When you remove judgement from the process, you allow for the natural (intrinsic) motivation to become more prominent, more potent. When you remove the judgement and the need for willpower, you will naturally start making incremental changes in your life, without forcing them.

HOW DOES
Transformation
HAPPEN?

*Pure logical thinking cannot yield us any knowledge
of the empirical world; all knowledge of reality
starts from experience and ends in it.*

— ALBERT EINSTEIN[11]

I have been in the industry of personal growth and transformation for over 20 years, and I can tell you with some confidence that I know how people's lives change. I've been witnessing it over years, not just the changes, but the stuckness and the confusion as well.

Among the most misplaced comments I've heard from my students are: "I already know that," "There is nothing new here," or a milder version of the same: "Thank you for reminding me about these truths!"

Now I want to share a secret with you in case you didn't know: Knowledge doesn't change a thing! Yes, I just said it: Knowledge doesn't change anything. It doesn't change your life.

And there is one more secret I want to share with you: the saying "What doesn't kill you makes you stronger" is wrong and dangerous.

With these two myths dispelled, let's dig deeper.

So, if knowledge doesn't change your life and experience doesn't necessarily make you stronger, what does?

Knowledge plus experience equals transformation. You need *both* knowledge and experience.

Experience alone will not necessarily give you the transformation you are seeking. It can make you stronger, but it can break you as well. If that myth were true, we would be living in a society of beautifully evolved and transformed human beings, because every single one of us has suffered in our own way. But the reality is different: there's a lot of anxiety, trauma, depression, and brokenness in the world. Because experience alone doesn't give you the kind of transformation you want.

What doesn't kill you may place you at a crossroads. You might actually become stronger, as the saying goes, but there is also a great risk of you becoming broken. Which one it will be depends on the framework: your values and beliefs, your skills and thought patterns, your support system. But ultimately, you need knowledge to make your experience work.

On the other hand, just having the knowledge doesn't change anything. Knowledge without experience is like a book on a shelf. It's only useful if you use it. And if you don't use it, its only function is to gather dust.

For knowledge to change your life, it has to shift from your mind into your heart: you have to experience it, live it, feel it. Here's an example:

You might have heard that "Happiness is in your hands." It is a beautiful, philosophical, and rather useless idea. For sure, happiness does depend on you, and if you look for it outside yourself, you are likely going to fail. But it is not a very useful idea in practical life. If you have an argument with your lover or if your child is sick, how much does it help you to search for happiness within?

Some years ago, my son Hayden had appendicitis. I picked him up from school because he was not feeling well. I was worried, so I took him to a doctor, and a few hours later they rushed my son into hospital for surgery. The one hour that I had to wait for Hayden to get out of surgery was absolutely excruciating. I kept pacing around the waiting room, worried and wondering why it was taking longer than anticipated. At that time, I could have been endlessly chanting, "Happiness is within me," and it would have been absolutely of no help. I just couldn't connect to the happiness within—it was an abstract idea that did not tie to my experience of being worried about someone I love so dearly.

A few months later, in the same year, I was driving to work and a song came on the radio. It was a popular dance piece, and it had a haunting refrain: "Everything will be okay." As I was listening to the music, I suddenly felt myself going back in time, as if I were 18 again— young, hopeful, carefree. This feeling was so strong, I didn't just imagine being young and hopeful, I felt it on a cellular level. At that very moment, I realised that no matter what happened to me, as long as I had myself, as long as I had my clear mind and was my real self, everything would be okay.

Suddenly, the idea that happiness really did come from within clicked into place. It suddenly made sense and was practical, usable, and relevant, because it had traveled from my mind into my heart. It moved from the realm of knowledge into the realm of experience.

And that, my friends, is how transformation happens: it is when your knowledge is lived through your experience, or when your experience is supported by your knowledge. But ultimately you will always need both.

Reflection Points

Let's take a moment for introspection. Think of any significant and emotionally charged event that has happened to you recently. It may be something pleasant or something painful. It may be a big life-changing event, such as meeting your life partner, or a trivial event, such as having a hard conversation with your boss.

Got it?

- How did this event make you feel? Can you name your emotions?

- What did this event highlight about your values, your needs, your wants, and your desires?

- What did this event highlight about you as a person, about your character?

- How did this event change or influence you as a person?

The point of this exercise is to help you bring introspection into your experiences and thus turn any event into a source of growth and transformation. You can do this exercise every time something significant or emotionally charged happens to you.

One

STEP

AT A TIME

It is only with the heart that one can see rightly;
what is essential is invisible to the eye.

— ANTOINE DE SAINT-EXUPÉRY [12]

So what if you genuinely have heard it all before? What if you're aware of all the varying theories of happiness and well-being: How do you change your life then?

There is a community of students in our niche who have this very problem. They have a problem and they want to solve it, so they buy courses, read books, attend events. They do it all and know it all, but the original problem stays the same.

Because when it comes to real life, especially if it is *your* life, where you are deep in it all, great ideas, wisdom, and simple truths don't always help. They don't work as well as they do *in theory*.

Why does this happen? Well, if life were so simple and came with a clear tutorial, if there were a recipe for a happy life, or a 10-things-to-do list to help us figure it all out, then we would all be happy and the world would be a beautiful place (or boring, who knows!).

But life doesn't have recipes, and there is no panacea or a universal remedy to fix all problems in personal growth. Not only do we need to find our own answers, but the right answers change as we do. They will evolve as we evolve. In other words, what works for me might not work for you, and what works for you now, might not work for you in five years' time.

It took me all those years to understand this simple truth: you cannot teach a person to climb a tree until they have learned to walk. Babies do not start walking on one beautiful day close to their first birthday. They first learn to hold their head up, then turn onto their tummy, then sit down, crawl, and only then are they ready to get up and walk (after a lot of falling down and getting up, and trying some more).

People, maybe even you, may not be ready to solve their problems on the spot. Even if you know all the wisdom, if you have heard all the answers, and even if you see what the solution is. If you're still stuck, if it still doesn't work nor make sense to you, maybe you are just at a different stage of the process.

Sometimes you need to learn to hold your head up and crawl before you take off climbing trees. Some problems need to be solved in stages or phases.

Solving a deeply painful problem is like peeling off layers of an onion. You'll get to the teary part, but first, you'll have to take off those old, dry outer layers.

It's like reading this book. If you're thinking that all of these ideas are great in theory, but you're struggling to apply them in real life because they are not quite applicable to you, because your situation is different, it is *special*, it has peculiar factors I am not aware of and thus makes your particular case a hard one to crack—well, it might just be that you've gone off to climb trees before you've learned to walk.

In that case, you have to start with step one and take it slow. Don't rush. Do step one as long as you need, until the outer layers start falling off and you start seeing your own situation a little more clearly, as if you are looking at it from a little distance.

And what's step one? Awareness. As I said, it all starts with awareness.

Reflection Points

You have worked through the first three parts of this book already. Good job! I know that this journey can be uncomfortable and unsettling. However, the best part of this book, the juiciest ideas and the greatest transformation are still ahead.

So your task at this point is going to be unexpected . . . but very important!

Take a break.

Go for a walk. Put everything aside. Get out of your head. Leave your phone behind and go for a solo walk.

Sometimes, all you need for a transformation to happen is a little pause, a little space, a little vacuum.

I'll see you in the next chapter!

PART IV

THE
ART OF
Imperfection

Who ARE YOU?

And identity is funny being yourself is funny
as you are never yourself to yourself except as you remember
yourself and then of course you do not believe yourself.

— GERTRUDE STEIN[1]

Who are you?

It isn't a philosophical question. I'm just asking about your basic regalia and accomplishments. If you were introduced on a show or at a networking event, what would be the short version of your bio, which would sum up your most important events and achievements?

Here's my example:

> I'm Kristina Mänd-Lakhiani, an author, teacher, entrepreneur, marketer, philanthropist, hobby farmer, artist, and everyday life philosopher. I'm also a proud mother, daughter, and friend.

That said, I am also many more things that would not fit into my official, short snippet of a bio. (Such things do, however, show up from time to time, depending on the circumstances.)

For the sake of simplicity, let's call all of those words in my bio my different "roles" that I play in life.[2] Sometimes I play the role of a teacher, but sometimes the role of a student. Sometimes I am an entrepreneur and a salesperson, and sometimes I am a customer.

Think of all the roles that you play in your life. There are many, and often they are polar opposites: teacher-student, child-parent, boss-subordinate, just to name a few.

And just like in theatre, roles come with their own scripts, costumes, masks, and acting. We show up differently in our different expressions. And even if the actor is essentially the same, we play out different characters, depending on the roles they have.

Now, let's take one of the professional roles in my repertoire—the role of the entrepreneur. When I go to a serious meeting where I need to come across as a reliable business partner, I put on a mask of professionalism. Not that I am not reliable or professional, but I don't need to show those qualities when I goof around with my children or even sit down to write. So it is a mask, because it is a layer I put over my natural self to play a certain role, or in more practical terms, to highlight a certain quality of my character.

When we play different roles, we put on different masks. Not that these masks are untrue, but they highlight certain qualities in our personalities and help us navigate the changing social landscape of our lives.

In fact, it is a great thing that we adjust our behaviour to changing or different circumstances. People who are not able to adjust to their environment, adhere to social norms, and consider the feelings of other people around them, are not usually pleasant company. Such behaviour, in its extreme expression, is classified as an antisocial personality disorder.

So, it is only natural that people learn to play different roles, adjust to their circumstances, and wear different
masks associated with those roles.

As soon as we start developing a sense of self at a very
early age, and acquire our first roles in life—as a child—we
start learning the rules of the game. When we are small,
we are told to behave, especially in public. "Put on this
nice dress; you are a girl." "Don't run around the restaurant; you are disturbing other diners." "Sit still and pay
attention; you are in school." "Be nice to these people;
they are our guests." And so it goes. We learn to modulate
our behaviour to our environment or circumstance.

In fact, at some point, a child figures out the game and
starts manipulating the different roles and different masks
to get what they want: "Mom, I'm upset because you didn't
let me climb that tree!" "You are such a nice friend. Can
you give me your toy?" Did you know that deception is an
important milestone in the psychological development of
a child?[3] It is just how our brain develops. Children learn
to present their case to their advantage, first awkwardly,
and later, as their cognitive abilities develop, with more
sophistication. (Deception and lying make for a curious
topic, and we'll pick this thread up in later chapters.)

As a child, you learn to modulate your behaviour to
your changing environment. You start trying on different
roles—a son or daughter, a spoiled grandchild, a friend,
a kindergartener, a student, a puppy owner, and so on.
Along with your social roles, you learn to wear another
layer of masks, to modulate your social roles—you can be
a good child, a naughty child, a curious child, a moody
child. And I'm not saying that these expressions are fake,
but we often wear our moods like a mask too (or hide them
behind one).

That said, you are not your emotions. Yet when you wear the mask of an emotion, just like with a costume, it starts dictating your behaviour.

Young children (and not so young, apparently) often resort to showing their emotions, or expressing them very vividly, even aggressively sometimes, because their verbal capacity to convey the extent, intensity, or particulars of their emotions is limited.[4] And so, from an early age, we learn to wear our emotions like an elaborate theatrical mask.

Naturally, with age, our vocabulary and emotional intelligence improve, and we are able to deal with our emotions with more wisdom and maturity. Curiously, however, we often keep resorting to the same old theatrical masks, which we learned to use when we were toddlers. "Mommy is sad because you didn't behave!" I confess, I'm guilty of this one—being vividly upset to drive the point. A few more examples: "I'm disappointed because you didn't meet my expectations," or the pinnacle of manipulation, "Shame on you! Look at how you made me feel!"

Have you ever worn an exaggerated, theatrical mask of an emotion, without actually feeling the emotion, or not feeling it to the extreme extent? For example, your child doesn't hear or heed your warning to be more careful and breaks a glass at mealtime. You want to make the point that "you should listen to your mother and behave accordingly." You are not really angry or upset because of the broken glass, but you have to make the point, and so you put on the mask of upsetness, or sternness, which is manipulative.

I don't even have a problem with manipulation, by the way. We all do it to a degree, not in an evil way, but yet we do it. We are sometimes extra nice, or extra stern, or a little more upset than we really are, or a little more interested.

We are all players in a big theatre, just as Shakespeare famously said, and it is only natural that we play our roles and wear our theatrical masks. After all, verbal communication is only responsible for about 7 percent of information exchange; the rest of the information is conveyed through vocal and visual communication,[5] our role, and mask.

But having emotions, wearing masks, and playing roles aren't the issue. The real problem arises when you start identifying yourself with them and forget who you truly are, who the real "you" is hiding behind those "decorations."

If you have ever been upset, you might identify with this scenario: your resentment is so long-standing and so exaggerated that when you try hard to remember why exactly you were upset in the first place, you cannot really recall or even understand how things blew out of proportion. This happens just as it did in childhood; that is, when words were not enough, we put on exaggerated masks of an emotion, and we played our roles wholeheartedly, trying to make a point, eventually believing our own drama.

So the real conundrum here is the act of identifying with our masks beyond the social circumstances where such masks belong.

- You end up carrying your favourite avatar everywhere you go:

- When you forget to take off your "successful entrepreneur and hustler" mask after you come home to your wife and children.

- When you are afraid to remove your armour of "Ms./Mr. Independent" with the people who truly love you.

When you forget who you really are—not your social roles, not your accomplishments, not your shiny regalia, not your righteous masks, but the real *you* . . . you have fallen into the trap. And getting out of it can be one of the biggest challenges you will ever face.

Reflection Points

This will be a fun exercise to get to know yourself a little better. Take a sheet of paper and list all the different (social) roles that you play in your life.

After you are done with the list, prioritise your roles. Mark your most important role with 1, then choose your second most important role and mark it with 2, and so on until the end of the list.

Finally, take a moment and write how you feel about each role. How important is it to you? Are you enjoying it? Does it make you feel good about yourself? Is it empowering you? What kind of emotions does this role evoke in you?

THE
PARADOX OF THE
Masks

*You can't wear a mask, Clark. When people see you and can
see the things you can do, the power you have, they'll be
terrified. They need to be able to look into your eyes, see your
face, so that they can see the decency and kindness that's
always there and know they have nothing to be afraid of.*

— MARTHA KENT[6]

So, what is your favourite mask?

Mine is the Good Girl.

I like to be a good girl. Friendly, polite, lively, positive,
smart, and absolutely definitely happy. This is my favourite and most useful mask. I use it when in doubt, when
I'm unsure, when I'm scared. (And when I genuinely feel
friendly, polite, lively, positive, smart, and absolutely definitely happy, ironically, I don't need to use it).

So why do we hide behind masks in the first place?

One of the biggest fears that we humans have is the
fear of rejection. In prehistoric times, early humans found
strength in one unique feature: their ability to form social
structures. Biologically, the human being is a lousy fighter
and easy prey for most predators. Yet we didn't become
extinct, did we? Far from it. We took over the planet and
dominated all other living creatures. Why? Because we
stuck together communicated, and passed valuable survival
information on to every new generation.

Our strength lies in our ability to be sociable. And in those early years of human history, being cast out of a social structure was a death sentence. Being banished from the tribe meant solitude, and solitude rendered us vulnerable to being eaten, dying of starvation, or getting killed by other tribes. Today, although that's no longer the case, our biological fear remains the same.

We might have gone far when it comes to knowledge, science, and technology. But our brain is pretty much the same as it was when we were still trying to figure out how to start a fire. And it reacts to the outside world just as it used to in prehistoric times.

So if your stress response to losing your car keys seems a little out of proportion, it is because your brain has been trained for hundreds of thousands of years to respond to any "threat" (e.g., losing your car keys) as it would if a predator were attacking. But don't demonise the brain: it is overreacting to save your life.

Today, we feel the same overwhelming fear, bordering on the fear of imminent death, when we experience rejection. This is how our biology is wired. There is nothing more natural.

And so, to avoid rejection (and the feeling of imminent death), you put on your "good girl" or "good boy" mask. You aim to please. It is such a natural need, to be liked by others, to belong,[7] and it is wired into us to always try to show others our best sides.

Remember any of your first dates? Russians call this the "candies and flowers season," when new romantic partners are on their best behaviour. The quirks and troubles come out later for both parties, because such "good behaviour" is not a sustainable long-term strategy.

And yet we sometimes waste our entire lives trying to hide our true selves behind a mask, whichever mask in your collection you deem socially acceptable and appropriate for a particular moment. We put on the masks to be liked and to be accepted, because our need to belong is biologically wired into us over thousands of years, and even the most unsocial hermit needs to be needed by someone, even if it is just a dog or a potted plant.

And here's the paradox. According to researcher Brené Brown,[8] you need three ingredients to form strong meaningful connections:

1. You have to believe that you are lovable the way you are.

2. You have to have courage to be imperfect.

3. You have to be vulnerable (the willingness to do something where there are no guarantees).

We put on the masks to be liked and accepted, yet to be truly liked and truly accepted we need to learn to take *off* our masks.

This is when your journey back to You really begins.

Reflection Points

This will be a simple, yet very powerful exercise. Look at yourself in the mirror and say the following words:

- "I am lovable. I am imperfect, I am flawesome, I am real, and I am lovable."

How did this simple exercise make you feel? Write down your thoughts, feelings, and realisations in your journal.

WHEN YOUR
Avatars
DON'T SEE EYE TO EYE

*We're built of contradictions, all of us. It's those opposing
forces that give us strength, like an arch,
each block pressing the next.*

— MARK LAWRENCE[9]

I have a sin to confess: I have a one-track mind.

If I do something, I do it wholeheartedly and focus all
my mental and physical efforts on the one task at hand.
It's like a deep dive under water—the outside world ceases
to exist. In general, it is not a bad quality: I can switch over
from one task to another, from one regime to another, and
be fully present with what I am doing at the moment.

If I'm on holiday, I am *on holiday.* My team may be a little upset with me when I don't answer the phone, but I am
not good at combining holidays with work. The same goes
for the times when I am at work. When I go on a business
trip, be it an event, networking, or shooting shows, I completely unplug from my everyday life back at home. And
then, a week later, sitting on a plane homeward bound, I
suddenly feel an overwhelming urge to see and hug my
kids again, because I was disconnected and didn't stay in
touch. And this is my sin—I plunge into work, and I forget
to call my kids, for days in a row.

And that is how my avatars start bickering at each other.
The Good Mom starts nagging the Busy Businesswoman:

"You are supposed to be a good mom. You love your kids. How can you forget to call them? What's wrong with you?!" And the Businesswoman feels ashamed, and a little confused: "I was trying to do my best, put all my hard work into the task at hand. I feel so bad for failing my kids."

The different social roles that we play are not always in sync. The actor is the same, but the scripts may be contradicting. And here lies the trap: Which role will take priority?

I have come across some curious research on the conflict of social roles.[10] It turns out that female leaders are often critically judged for displaying qualities of a good leader, because such qualities contradict what society expects women to be. If we believe that good leaders are assertive and focused on the task, yet we believe that women are compassionate and focused on social dynamics, then the two expectations are obviously in conflict (which, by the way, is not the case for men). And it turns out that gender roles take priority over leadership roles in general perception. And so women get harshly judged for failing their gender stereotypes, while exhibiting the qualities of a good leader.

Something similar happens in your head when your two avatars don't see eye to eye:

- When the Entrepreneur in you is in conflict with the Parent in you, such as in my earlier example.

- When the Boss in you is in conflict with the Friend in you, such as when you need to communicate a hard decision and you are afraid to hurt someone else's feelings. In years of running a business, I've had to communicate a lot of unpleasant news and hard decisions, such as when I had to let go of half of our team and, naturally, some of the people I've had to fire over the years were friends, and some of them still are. But when you are facing the obvious decision that you have to let go of someone on your team because they do not thrive, do not contribute, have lost interest, but you also feel emotionally engaged because that someone is a friend, the two social roles in you, the Boss and the Friend, will have a nasty fight.

- When the Human in you is in conflict with the Hero in you, or whatever society expects of you, like in the case with Simone Biles when she prioritised her well-being over being a national hero during the 2021 Olympics. Simone's case is a vivid example of how devastating the conflict may become when some of your social roles are running on contradictory scripts.

Any two of your roles may turn out to be contradictory and give you a nasty internal conflict to resolve. So I ask again, which of your roles is going to take priority? But more importantly, if one of the roles will take priority, how do you deal with the deprioritised role? Will the Parent in you feel shame for prioritising business? Will the Friend in you suffer? Will you be taken off the pedestal if you prioritise the Human over the Hero?

I think the real problem is not that our roles are sometimes contradictory. That, in fact, is quite natural. The problem is when you cannot come to peace with the roles you had to temporarily deprioritise. It's when you feel shame for the personal choices you are making and, rather than moving on with your decision, keep being stuck in the guilt and shame of not being a good enough Parent, a good enough Friend, the real Hero, a good enough _____ (fill in the blank).

Reflection Points

In the next few days, pay attention to the different social roles that you play in your everyday life. Pay special attention to situations when you are playing multiple roles simultaneously—a parent and a professional, a working colleague and a friend, etc.

Notice when your roles are in conflict and pay attention to your priorities. Which role do you prioritise instinctively? How does it make you feel about the deprioritised role?

You can write down your discoveries and realisations in your diary.

YOU CANNOT *Shame* YOURSELF OUT OF BEING YOU

Wisdom is tolerance of cognitive dissonance.

— PROF. ROBERT A. F. THURMAN[11]

Cognitive dissonance[12] is my favourite little birdie that comes to announce a change. It's when your feelings are contradictory, and you are suddenly confused: *What is going on with me?* For example:

- When you hear the news you most feared, but you suddenly feel relieved rather than devastated.

- When you lose your job, rather than feeling disappointed or worried about the future, you feel excited for the new opportunities.

- When you are praised and celebrated, but you feel uncomfortable and out of place, like a fraud or an impostor, rather than feeling proud.

- When you divorce a turbulent marriage, and you suddenly feel warmth and friendship toward a person who used to drive you nuts.

- When you say your last good bye to an elderly relative, but as opposed to feeling depressed, you feel a sense of lightness because their

earthly journey and suffering is over and all you
are left with are beautiful, loving memories.

- When you discover that you have been played
and betrayed and, rather than feeling broken or
bitter, you feel relieved to finally see the truth.

- When you summon the courage to part ways
with your business partner or friend, and
suddenly feel that you have wings behind your
back, rather than feeling lost and scared.

- When you have to give up a big goal and admit
defeat, but rather than feeling a loss, you feel
excitement because you are now free to pursue
new dreams.

- When you finally achieve a big goal, wake
up in your dream, but you feel empty and
apathetic rather than feeling ecstatic, as you had
predicted.

It was with these kinds of "wrong feelings" and
"wrong thoughts" that my real journey to self-discovery
and transformation started. They were like a glitch in the
matrix: every time I felt something I was not supposed
to feel, the whole illusion would quiver, and I could not
ignore the effect. Eventually, I had to dig in and figure out
what was going on.

I once wrote a social media post in which I was trying
to make a point about acceptance, taking the world and
people as they are, and I shared a personal experience I
had been going through. I was not feeling well that day,
emotionally nor physically, and I wanted help and support.
I wanted to be seen in my pain. Yet, my then-husband,
Vishen, was busy with his own endeavours, and I felt
what I felt—disappointed, unimportant, and not heard. I
described my inner conflict in this letter to my followers.

I did conclude that it was my job to accept my situation. I thought I had done a good job of introspection and personal transformation, moving away from victimhood. Little did I know that the real introspection and transformation came later, when I saw the responses to my post.

I got piles of angry responses with one simple message: "You should be proud of your remarkably successful husband and not disappointed that he didn't help! Stop whining and just do what you are supposed to do: take care of your family and your home. That's your job and there's nothing to complain about."

The Good Girl in me caught on to the criticism—it seemed just and fair. Of course I have to do what I have to do, and what's the point in feeling anything but grateful? But the Human in me was feeling even less important, even less heard. Should I really be ashamed of my feelings?!

It took several more years and many more glitches in the matrix for me to finally realise that I was simply tired of feeling ashamed of my feelings, thoughts, or just being me. You cannot shame yourself out of feeling whatever it is that you are feeling. Emotions simply don't work like that.

The bad news is that nobody teaches us how to feel. We often hear how *not* to feel: "Don't cry!" "Don't be so upset over nothing!" "Don't be disappointed!" "Don't be angry!" "Don't be dramatic!" But just because someone tells you not to feel something doesn't mean that you will stop feeling it. It's not like you have a switch for your emotions. So how do you feel your feels *properly*?

The good news is that humankind has an answer to this question. It's no mystery, no magic; it's simply psychology. Susan David, a brilliant scientist, psychologist, and a TED speaker, provides a simple algorithm for dealing with complicated emotions in her book, *Emotional*

Agility,[13]. She proposes that we start by quitting the judgements we have regarding our emotions.

There are no good or bad emotions, Susan David suggests. There are no positive or negative emotions. Emotions just *are*, and each emotion has a role to play.

I like to compare our emotional body with our physical body. Human bodies have an ability to feel physical pain. There is a very clear reason why we feel pain—this is the way our body signals that something is wrong, that some part of our body requires attention or healing. For example, when you touch a hot surface, you feel pain and pull your hand away. There is a medical condition when people do not feel physical pain: congenital analgesia.[14] People with this condition usually die in childhood from injuries and unnoticed diseases, because their bodies do not have the ability to signal that something is wrong. Simply put, without the signal, the body breaks and deteriorates because it is not getting the healing and attention it requires.

Just like the physical sensations that help us keep our bodies safe and healthy, we have emotions that help us keep our lives balanced and thriving. Your emotion is a signal: "Hey, pay attention! Something is going on here!" And just like with physical sensations, you need to apply appropriate measures to make sure that you take care of yourself and remain safe and healthy. You don't just slap a Band-Aid on anything that doesn't feel good with your body. You don't just pop a paracetamol (acetaminophen)[15] whenever something new and intense hurts inside. You know that to stay healthy you need to eliminate the cause of the pain, not just its symptoms.

Yet, when it comes to our emotional bodies, we often resort to Band-Aids and paracetamols—quick fixes to the unpleasant sensations, leaving the causes not only untreated, but often undetected, hidden in the depths of the subconscious. And over time we feel stress, anxiety, and depression, and we cannot answer the only real question: *Why?* What was the real cause of feeling low, apathetic, uninspired, angry, stuck, anxious, stressed, scared, or depressed?

I believe that the biggest problem of contemporary society is emotional analgesia. We learn to ignore emotional pain, focusing on the positive and demanding good vibes only, slapping on Band-Aids, and popping paracetamols to feel better, while our lives break and deteriorate from undetected trauma.

Reflection Points

This is another twist to the awareness exercise, which we started in Part III. Anchor your moments of awareness to intense emotions. Every time you feel an intense emotion, take a pause for a few moments, and ask yourself:

- What am I feeling now? Name your emotion.
- Do I like my feeling, or would I prefer to feel different in this situation?
- If your answer to the previous question is "I don't like what I am feeling," ask yourself, Why do you feel that way?

As usual, avoid judgement and approach this exercise with curiosity.

Defence
MECHANISMS:
WE ALL HAVE THEM

Self-deception is a defining part of our human nature.
By recognizing its various forms in ourselves and reflecting
upon them, we may be able to disarm them and even,
in some cases, to employ and enjoy them.

— NEEL BURTON[16]

Would you like to learn how to deal with your emotional pain? Would you like to toss away your stash of emotional Band-Aids? I wholeheartedly believe that we should have been taught emotional first aid at a very early age, in primary school, because it is one of the most useful skills for life. And it is not rocket science.

Susan David's idea that we should not judge our emotions as good or bad, positive or negative, right or wrong, begs the question: How do we work with them?

Since nobody ever taught us how to work with our emotions, naturally, we are challenged to figure it out on our own. And when we have to figure something out without help or guidance, the only thing we can go by is our natural instinct. And that, I believe, is why so many of us resort to incredibly maladaptive coping strategies, or defence mechanisms,[17] when we face an unpleasant sensation.

Let me paint you a few simple scenes from everyday life to illustrate how it works.

Imagine having an unresolved conflict with a colleague. Maybe your colleague does not stick to deadlines, or passes sloppy work to you, or you disagree on some important professional issue, or you simply don't like their style of communication. You feel irritated and justly expect the colleague to do better, to keep to deadlines and produce better quality work. What do you do? Do you tell your colleague how you feel about their performance?

A lot of people would keep quiet just because they don't like conflict and confrontation. Or they may be afraid of their unpleasant colleague turning the tables and attacking them in response to their criticism. Some people choose to voice their concerns, but the fight may turn out to be really ugly. And then you turn the argument over in your head, ruminate, and feel bad for even bringing it up. Alternatively, your colleague may ignore your criticism. You might be giving this feedback to them over and over again with no result. What happens next? Most likely, your resentment and animosity will grow. You might give up criticising your colleague's work, but you will start backstabbing them for seemingly unrelated reasons, pointing out the flaws in their character to others.

I could go on painting this picture for a few more pages, but I want to draw your attention to this: most of those natural and normal reactions that I mentioned in the scenario above—avoiding conflict, turning the tables, escalating animosity, ruminating, resentment, and emotional leakage, etc.—are maladaptive coping strategies. In other words, they may give you temporary relief, but they do not solve the underlying problem.

As you see, most of the natural reactions that we have learned over the years are not really so helpful. These are the Band-Aids, and the paracetamols that we keep applying to much deeper wounds, which keep trickling poison into our everyday life. In my line of work, this is called "emotional or spiritual bypassing," but in more professional terms, we are talking about defence mechanisms.

There are quite a few defence mechanisms out there, and I will illustrate some examples now. I wonder if you relate to any of these reactions:

- When the COVID-19 pandemic began, many people, myself included, could not believe that the situation was so serious, the virus was so dangerous, and that quarantines, lockdowns, and isolation would last so long. We put our plans on hold, pushed them back by a few months, and then a few more, and then a little more, and then, finally, we accepted that the world had changed. When we are faced with a very unpleasant reality, we are tempted to argue against it, refuse to see the most anxiety-provoking and threatening aspects of it, deny its seriousness and its very existence. This defence mechanism is called (not surprisingly) **denial**.

- Another curious outcome of the 2020 pandemic was the extreme polarisation of society on nearly every aspect of the crisis. Some people passionately defended the brutality and deadliness of the virus, others passionately claimied that the virus was nothing more than a seasonal flu, and those who claimed that it did not exist at all. There were people passionately promoting vaccination against the virus and others passionately fighting against it. And the curious detail was that each camp had a wealth of (what they call) facts, empirical data, evidence, and arguments to defend their cases. It was almost as if parallel reality bubbles coexisted in society. It is a natural tendency to reshape our external reality to meet our internal needs in such anxiety-provoking situations. This defence mechanism is called *distortion.*

- Let's switch gears to something a little less provoking and polarising and come back to my earlier example of a conflict with a colleague. Sometimes your problematic colleague might not say anything openly, might not criticise or attack you directly, but you do notice that something is wrong, because they show their frustration in more passive ways: they may be stubborn, uncooperative, snappy, difficult, slow. This is an example of another defence mechanism—*passive-aggressive behaviour.*

- The next one is curious and a little tricky. Have you ever felt righteous about something? Or hypervigilant about other people's behaviour? I remember sharing a flat with a friend who used to get angry every time I had male friends over for a visit. He thought I was behaving wrongly and promiscuously. In his opinion, I could not have innocent male friends, and so he judged and condemned me for something that, in my opinion, was not my sin. I don't want to make assumptions about the reasons behind my friend's judgement, but often, when we have subconscious, unacknowledged, and unacceptable urges and desires, rather than dealing with such unwanted emotions, we project them onto other people. This often manifests itself as jealousy, prejudice, and hypervigilance. This defence mechanism is called *projection.*

- Have you ever lashed out at someone, maybe even treated someone unjustly, and then apologised, sharing that you had had a very hard day? This is a common transgression, and it is an understandable reaction. However, in its more extreme form, you might find yourself habitually grumpy or unfriendly with your spouse or your children because you are under huge stress at work. This defence mechanism is called **displacement**, and its simplest expression is this: you kicked a cat because your boss was a jerk to you.

• Here is another reaction to a jerk-boss: you might act as if you really like your boss. In simple terms, rather than dealing with the conflict with your unpleasant boss, you convince yourself that you really like them and act out in an exaggerated manner. Or the opposite of this: if you are in a committed relationship and you feel attracted to someone else, you might convince yourself and act out that you dislike and disapprove of that attractive person. This defence mechanism is called **reaction formation:** this is one of my favourite phenomena because it is such a trickster.

This is not a comprehensive list, obviously. Different schools of psychology have different lists and classifications of defence mechanisms.[18] The ones listed above are quite common and easy to understand, but you can go deeper studying this topic if you find it as fascinating as I do.

The classification that I used here is based on the work of George E. Vaillant,[19] who categorises defence mechanisms by the level of their maturity, meaning that not all defence mechanisms are bad. Some are pathological, like denial or distortion, but most are simply immature, which means that there is no big harm in occasionally reacting in such ways to stressful and anxiety-provoking situations. The problem arises when they become predominant, when you don't move from reactive behaviour to adaptive strategies.

Here it is again: there are no absolutes. Something may be good for you in a particular situation, but it may turn out bad for you if you misuse it. There are practises and strategies that are good for you, but if you overuse or misuse them, they may create more problems. Too much of a good thing becomes bad, even glorified concepts and experiences, such as love and positivity.

Reflection Points

Let's take a moment for introspection. You can use your journal to write down your answers.

- Can you think of situations in the past when you were using any of the above defence mechanisms?

- Which of the defence mechanisms do you resort to most often?

- What would be a more productive way to respond to recurring triggering situations in your life?

A WEAPON
OF
Love

Ironically, it can be hard to discern the truth in a group of apparent truth seekers. I've hung with New Age authors who were just plain mean and addicted to their image. And . . . I've been to a few AA meetings with friends, and man, was it ever refreshing. People were just upfront about being messed up.

— DANIELLE LAPORTE[20]

I have a somewhat complicated relationship with love. Don't get me wrong—I appreciate the feeling. But in a way, despite its simplicity, it is one very loaded buzzword with a huge amount of baggage. This chapter is not about love per se, but I'll just use it as an example, because, without doubt, in its purest form, love is good.

So, when someone says "I love you" and it doesn't feel quite right, you are bound to experience cognitive dissonance.

Here are a few simple examples:

I remember getting into a heated discussion with a woman on social media. I disagreed with something she had said and expressed it with as much tact and respect as I could muster. I did have respect for the woman and her work, so I put in a sincere effort. She argued back and I responded. It quickly escalated, and after a few heated remarks on both sides, the woman switched to "I have only love for you!" I tried to get some clarity, and I have to admit that I was becoming emotional despite all attempts to keep it cool. But the woman kept blasting me with different versions of "I have only love for you."

On the receiving end, it felt eerie, menacing, and a bit threatening. Needless to say, rather than "calming down," I felt increasingly uncomfortable. Our argument didn't end in any logical conclusion. She kept blasting me with "love," and I gave up trying to get any sense out of the conversation, so I walked away.

This isn't an isolated event. Have you come across such highly spiritual replies (for lack of a better word) to unpleasant comments on social media? I am a little bit of a prude myself, and I like to cut off rude comments with a polite "Excuse me, but such comments are not welcome here," so I understand the strategy of not getting involved. But there are nuances. There is a difference between ignoring random trolls, which is generally a wise choice of action, and muting out one's personal acquaintances and friends, which is called *stonewalling* and is, in fact, a defence mechanism.

A more subtle nuance lies in the difference between a dry and civil "such comments are unwelcome" and a very loaded "I have only love for you." Such professions of love in the context of a conflict can sound almost menacing.

Don't get me wrong—I have experienced contradictory feelings of strongly disagreeing with someone and still having great respect, even love, for the person. Respect is the crucial word here. I can express love with respect. If there is no respect, as you see in mindless trolling, then the maximum I can offer is civility.

Here is a slightly different take on the same misuse of the word *love*: I had a friend, let's call her Carol,[21] who was one of the sweetest people imaginable. She showered everyone with love, which she was very outspoken about, little gifts and notes of attention and general sweetness of manner. So it was a little surprising when I first felt that some of her naive comments were hurtful. I wrote it off to her sweet and naive nature: "Maybe she just doesn't realise how I am looking at it?" But the stabs kept coming, and I started noticing that I was subconsciously avoiding girl-dates with Carol because I wasn't entirely sure if one of her careless comments might hurt me.

And, oh boy, did they hurt! But it didn't end there. After a few initial, naive stabs came other tricks and odd, inexplicable situations, which left me feeling totally wrong in a strange and vague manner. It was a few years later that I came across the topic of psychopathic and manipulative behaviour and recognised passive aggression, gaslighting, triangulation, and a plethora of dirty tricks.

When I finally became sufficiently suspicious, I asked Carol if she was upset with me. I must have hurt her in some way. So I suggested that she tell me how she really felt. I was willing to hear the criticism and make the necessary corrections. But what I heard in reply left me baffled—with an innocent smile, she said: "But, Kristina, I love you!"

You see, the problem with such scenarios is that the feeling that something is wrong is so subtle, you can barely put your finger on it. And when I write down those examples in plain words, I almost feel wrong—"What's the matter with me? Maybe these people are genuinely angelic, and I am the one who is deviant?"

Well, the truth is, that apart from such feelings of doubt and guilt being a natural reaction to manipulation, such expressions of passive aggression are hard to call out, because they are masked behind a very noble feeling—love.

Love ceases to be love when used as a mask or a shield, or when wielded as a weapon. Now, *that* is a pure misuse of love.

Naturally, it is not only love that can be used as a shield for manipulation and defence mechanisms. You can use joy, peace, balance, and awakening as great excuses to distance yourself from unpleasant emotions. And that is exactly what spiritual bypassing means.

In the words of John Welwood, a psychotherapist and a Buddhist teacher who came up with the term in the 1980s, *spiritual bypassing* is a "tendency to use spiritual ideas and practises to sidestep or avoid facing unresolved emotional issues, psychological wounds, and unfinished developmental tasks."[22]

The problem here is that your dragons will not cease to exist, no matter how well you build the walls of spirituality around them. Even the holiest of people have human emotions, and any sort of obsession with non-attachment, emotional analgesia, and being above everything human is not only strange, but simply dangerous for your well-being.

The extra special problem with spiritual bypassing is not only the fact that the person is engaging in harmful maladaptive behaviour, but it is also extremely damaging to other people.

Here are just a few consequences of spiritual bypassing that are harmful to others:

- It leads to dismissing other people's emotions. "Why are you angry?" "You are so negative!" "Don't be so jealous!" "You need to go align yourself."

- It may lead to avoiding your personal responsibility. "I am fine. You are the one who is crazy!"

- It may lead to judging other people and even spiritual narcissism. "I am better than you because I practise spirituality / I meditate / I do yoga / I don't drink alcohol."

- It may lead to justifying extreme cases of suffering. "It is God's will." "Everything happens for a reason."

If you have been on the receiving end of spiritual bypassing, you probably understand why I am so passionate about this particular phenomenon. I'll be blunt: this is my personal pain speaking, and helplessness, since it is so hard to call out someone so righteous, enlightened, and holy. And on a philosophical level they may be right—everything does happen, whether for a reason or not, but you must make the best of it.

And that is what we are going to talk about next. So, if you are ready to give up your defence mechanisms and maladaptive coping strategies, let's talk about emotional first aid: How do you make the best of whatever life throws at you?

Reflection Points

This is a simple yet powerful tool for you. I want you to pay attention to situations when you doubt or discount your own feelings.

Maybe somebody says that you are too dramatic or over-reacting; maybe someone points out that you are more blessed than many others, and hence you have no right to feel low; maybe you feel guilty or apologetic for your real feelings.

When you notice that you "wrong" your emotions, or doubt your own reason, say to yourself:

- "This is how I feel, and I have the right to feel the way I do."

Acknowledge your real emotion and allow it to be. However, make sure that you do not make any rash decisions or get into arguments while your emotions are intense. We are going to talk about proper ways to process your painful emotions in the following chapters. This exercise aims only at giving you permission to feel whatever you feel without guilt, shame, or doubt.

EMOTIONAL

First Aid

Discomfort is the price of admission to a meaningful life.

— SUSAN DAVID[23]

I believe that the path back to you starts with emotional well-being. Emotional well-being is coming to peace with the full spectrum of our expressions, with all our experiences and every emotion. It is then that we are ready to return to who we truly are.

Emotional intelligence is the central piece in this puzzle. And while all my previous examples were about your relationships with the world and other people, true emotional intelligence is about learning to be at peace with yourself.

So, if in all those earlier examples you replace the object, or the "other person" with yourself, you will see how everything clicks into place. We'll come back to this idea at the very end of my book, but for now, let's move on to emotional first aid, that skill that "they"[24] failed to teach us in early childhood.

The following is my own seven-step formula for working with painful emotions. It is based on the works of various authors and my own observations, experience, and practise. As usual, I encourage you to dig deeper and learn more on the topic, but for the purpose of this book, I'm giving you a simple algorithm. And a disclaimer—if you have persistent and seemingly unresolvable emotional issues or past traumas, you must seek the help of a professional psychotherapist. Self-medication is not good when it comes to your emotional well-being, just as you wouldn't try to fix your broken leg on your own.

Here is my algorithm for working with painful emotions:

Be Aware ➤ Acknowledge ➤ Locate ➤ Name ➤ Diagnose ➤ Relax ➤ Release

1. Be aware—notice the emotion.
2. Acknowledge the emotion.
3. Locate the emotion in your body.
4. Name the emotion.
5. Diagnose—What is this emotion telling you?
6. Relax physically.
7. Release the emotion.

The whole process does not take a lot of time, and you could practise this sequence anytime, anywhere—well, as long as you keep practicing it. We are now going to look deeper into each step of this sequence, but as a side note, this sequence is only meant for processing immediate emotions. If you are interested in a wider context of working with your emotions, I suggest you begin with Susan David's work.[25]

1. BE AWARE

A surprising reason why we are so clumsy with our emotions is a lack of awareness. Simply put: people don't even realise that they are going through various emotions during the day. They just know that they are stressed, depressed, or stuck, but it is like thick brown fog with no clear outlines or details.

I was doing a class on emotional literacy one day and asked participants to share which emotions they were feeling. One woman replied: "I'm going through a rough patch in my life right now, but I don't really feel anything. No emotions."

A complete absence of emotions is not very likely. We feel emotions most of the time while we are awake, but not all of them are intense or even familiar enough to be named or recognised. Similarly to your physical body, you might be used to describing an absence of pain or intense sensations as "not feeling anything." But if you were to shift your focus to your own physical body, you would suddenly notice light and unobtrusive sensations, such as the air and its temperature, the touch of your clothes on your skin, maybe even your heartbeat.

What could be hiding behind "I'm not feeling anything" may be even more concerning—apathy, disillusionment, resignation. Such emotions, even if they are at an early and mild stage, need to be noticed.

And so the first step of this sequence is paying attention. You have to start with awareness if you want to improve your emotional well-being. Notice what is going on.

Emotions are fluid by nature—they flow and change like water in a river. Unless you obstruct the flow of that river, in which case your emotions will get stuck and, just like water, start "stinking,"[26] your emotions will keep flowing and changing.

A simple way to start is to pay attention to your emotions throughout the day. And, to make it really work, start an Emotional Diary—write them down.

2. ACKNOWLEDGE

This is usually the hardest step for most Good Girls and Good Boys who have a clear picture of what it means to be the perfect version of themselves. And I'll put it bluntly:

once you start doing this work, you will notice emotions you didn't realise you had the capacity to feel. In fact, you will notice emotions you think are beneath you to experience, which you would like to condemn, eliminate, ban.

But remember the first simple rule of emotional intelligence: emotions are neither good nor bad, neither right nor wrong. They just *are,* and they carry an important message for you.

Some emotions will be unpleasant and even feel unacceptable, but here is the important nuance: if you don't acknowledge or accept your emotions, it is like obstructing the flow of a river. Those emotions will get stuck in your subconscious, and they will not disappear. They will start "stinking." In more scientific terms, it will lead to either an unexpected and inappropriate explosion of suppressed emotions or to "emotional leakage"—involuntarily exposing emotions, either verbally or nonverbally.

So the best you can do is remove the obstruction and let the emotion flow. Surprisingly, when emotions flow, they change. And since emotions are fluid by nature and have a tendency to change, you also realise something else that is pretty revolutionary: you are not your emotions; you are just the one experiencing them.

- If you are feeling angry, it doesn't mean that you are an angry person.

- If you are feeling uninspired, it doesn't mean that you are a dull or stupid person.

- If you are feeling ashamed or guilty, it doesn't mean that you are a flawed person.

Have you ever experienced a sudden swing of emotions? You might have gotten upset with someone rude on a street and then bumped into your good friend and suddenly felt joy. You are angry one moment and friendly the next—you are the same human being experiencing different emotions.

It might be helpful to change your language a little to make this step of the process easier. Express your emotions through "I feel . . ." rather than "I am . . ." See the difference? "I **feel** angry," rather than "I **am** angry."

3. LOCATE

Every emotion expresses itself somewhere in your body, and that is how we know that something is going on.

- If you are afraid, you might feel dizzy or nauseous, your legs might be trembling, your hands might be sweating, and your voice might quiver.

- If you feel sad or grieved, you might feel heaviness in your chest, your head might feel foggy, and you might have difficulty breathing.

- If you feel joy, you might feel physically lighter and more energetic, your head might feel clearer, and your physical senses might be sharper.

The point is that every emotion expresses itself in one way or another in your body. And, to be clear, it is an individual process, so your anger and my anger might feel very different in our respective bodies.

So, pay attention to your body and locate your emotion—How does it express itself in your body? Which part of your body does it reside in? How does it feel? Notice your body, your breath, your physical senses, your mind—different emotions impact various aspects of our biology in different ways. Noticing the physical component of your emotions is a great skill to work with later on.

4. NAME

The next important step in the process is to pinpoint your emotion, give it a precise and nuanced name. It is an interesting technique, and it has a couple of huge benefits.

First, the more precisely you name your emotions, the easier it is to process them. The more universal a name you give to your emotions, the harder it is to deal with them. I'll give a somewhat funny analogy to get the idea across. If you had to eat an elephant, it would be very difficult to imagine the task as a whole.[27] So, according to the idiom, you have to eat an elephant piece by piece. The more precisely you name the emotion, the smaller the slice of an elephant you are dealing with.

If you say, "I am feeling depressed," it is such a wide and vague concept, it is hard to start working on it, just like eating a big elephant. But if you pinpoint to a more nuanced emotion, for example, that you're feeling disappointed, or demoralised, or dejected, the task at hand becomes clearer. You are not dealing with a vague umbrella concept, "depression," but with a specific aspect of it.

The second advantage of such an approach is that it helps to train your emotional intelligence to be more aware of the variety, nuances, and intensity of human emotions.

Let's do a little mental experiment. Think of as many emotions as you can come up with on the spot. You can even write them down on a piece of paper. Most people can think of a dozen so-called primary emotions and then expand a little deeper. It is hard, however, to go beyond 50 emotions from the top of your head. In the appendix, there's a chart with over 300 nuanced emotions to start working with.[28] But I'm sure this is not the limit.

5. DIAGNOSE

The nature of emotions is rather simple—they arise in response to events, they make themselves known physically in our body, and they carry important information. Once you "receive" the information, the emotion will "move on."

So this step is crucial for your emotional well-being. You have to hear what the emotion has to tell you. Only when you hear what the emotion has to tell you, will it move on, because it would have served its purpose.

If you suppress your emotion or ignore its message, it will keep repeating itself until one of two things happens—you get the message and start working on the cause of your unwanted emotions, or you break from untreated emotional wounds.

At this step, you need to ask yourself a few simple questions:

- What is this emotion telling me?
- Which of my values might this emotion highlight?
- Which of my beliefs might this emotion highlight?
- Which of my characteristics might this emotion highlight?

For example, if you were criticised at work and it caused you to feel unworthy or insecure, you might realise that you are doubting your own abilities, that you have unrealistic expectations of excellence, and your job is extremely important to you.

Or if you feel rattled and confused because you had an argument with your loved one, you might realise the importance of this relationship for you and your own fears or insecurities in relation to this person.

Naturally, you will need courage, honesty, and kindness toward yourself to complete this step properly, and we will talk about these qualities in Parts V, VI, and VII. But keep in mind that this step is about clarity and honesty, and, at this point in time, you do not need to understand the wider context of what is happening.

For now, your goal is to relieve your emotional pain or its intensity. Once you are feeling better, you will be fit to deal with the wider context and create an action plan to move on or deal with the causes of your pain. Here's another analogy: if you get injured in an accident, your doctor will first need to stop the bleeding and get your vitals under control, and then they will be ready to treat the injury. In psychology, it works just the same: You don't deal with the problem on the same level of mental state on which the problem occurred. You first need to become calm and composed.

And that is what we are now ready to do.

6. RELAX

You might have experienced how emotions express themselves in the physical body—you feel each emotion in a certain part of your body. The stronger the emotion, the more intense the physical sensation is.

And the good news is that the reverse causality also works: if you relax your body physically, your emotions subside and, eventually, disappear.

I will not tire of repeating, however, that this sequence is emotional first aid. You will have to work with the wider context and the root causes of your emotions later, when you are in a better state. While this technique might give you real physical and emotional relief, it alone is not enough, so make sure that you don't use it as yet another defence (or escape) strategy.

You located the emotion you are working with in your physical body in step three of this sequence. Now shift your attention back to your body and focus on that particular part where you are feeling the emotion. Now, tell that part of your body to relax. Literally, give your body the verbal command to relax physically.

When people feel pain or discomfort, they tense up. It is our natural response to pain.

Counterintuitively, what you really need to do to ease the pain is the exact opposite: relax. Focus on physical relaxation. If relaxing the tension or letting go of the pain is hard, focus on relaxing your body overall. Relax those parts that you can and imagine how relaxation spreads throughout your body and eventually takes over even the most tensed muscles and tissues.

It also helps to relax your face. Feel the tissues around your eyes relax, give your face a faint smile, relax your jaw, and unclench your teeth. Relax your shoulders, your hips.

Finally, focus on your breathing. Breathe deeply and rhythmically. You can practise the box breathing technique, which is particularly good for restoring balance:

1. Breathe in to the count of 4.

2. Hold your breath to the count of 4.

3. Breathe out to the count of 4.

4. Hold your breath to the count of 4.

Repeat this technique for a few rounds.

Box Breathing Technique

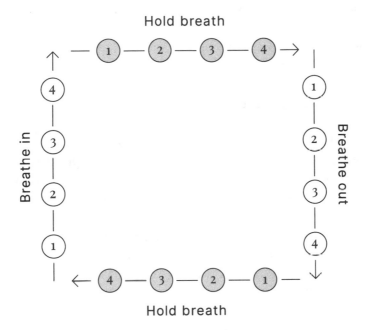

Focusing on your physical sensations and actively relaxing will not only help you let go of tension and physical discomfort, but it will also shift your attention away from the painful emotions for a brief respite.

7. RELEASE

Now you are ready for the final step: to release your emotion.

While relaxing physically is easy to understand and fairly simple to achieve with a few hacks (relaxing specific muscles, breathing), letting go of your painful emotion may seem a little puzzling. For this process, you are going to use your imagination.

If your primary mode of perception is visual, you can visualise your emotion as an object—a dark cloud, a heavy rock, or any symbol that resonates with you. Imagine how you can entice this object representing your emotion to leave your body: you may imagine blowing on a cloud until it dissolves, dropping a heavy rock to the bottom of the ocean, or taking a sponge and erasing the object representing your emotion, as if it were a picture on a blackboard.

If you are not very visual and your primary sense is auditory, then use words to help you in the process. You can say to the emotion: "I'm letting you go. Thank you for showing up and giving me this information. Your job is done; now you can go."

If you are more drawn to the sense of touch, then keep focusing on the physical sensation of calm, balance, peace, lightness, relief, whatever you may feel as a result of releasing your painful emotion. Feel that soothing new emotion in your body, feel it physically, intensify it, and let it spread throughout your body.

Whatever works for you, use it. And make sure you write about your experience in your Emotional Diary. According to social psychologist James Pennebaker, who has researched journaling for over 40 years, writing about traumatic experiences helps process painful emotions. Furthermore, there's a lot of research linking journaling to improved sleep, stronger immunity, and better overall health.[29]

Reflection Points

This is another useful twist to the awareness exercise, which I introduced in Part III of this book ("Escaping the Rut"). I hope you keep doing it as agreed, for 30 days.

In this new iteration of the exercise, rather than focusing on the present moment, you will focus on your emotions: every time your alarm rings, pay attention to your present emotion. It may be a little hard in the beginning, especially if you are not used to noticing your emotions, but you will get better with practise.

Ask yourself these questions:

- What am I feeling right now?
- How strong is this emotion?
- Is it an intense emotion, a mood, or just a faint feeling?
- With the help of the "Expanded Emotional Vocabulary," which is provided in the Appendix, pick a precise name for your emotion.

Don't judge your emotion as "good" or "bad," but ask yourself if you would like to feel more of this emotion, less of this emotion, or if you are indifferent about it.

I suggest you write down your observations in your journal. It will help you to put even vague and barely perceptible feelings into words.

NO ONE WANTS YOUR
Perfection

The tyrant dies and his rule is over,
the martyr dies and his rule begins.

— SØREN KIERKEGAARD[30]

I was 40 when I realised that I was done being ashamed of who I am. I was done feeling ashamed for what I felt and for all those things I didn't allow myself to feel. Shame was not doing me any good.

I was feeling ashamed for feeling lost, sad, confused, for not being happy and proud of my life to the extent I was supposed to. But how was I supposed to feel? My BS-barometer just peaked at around that time, and I realised that all the imaginary claims of the world on what I am and what I am not were complete nonsense. And the key word here is *imaginary* because, really, the world didn't care about me, and even less about my emotions.

Naturally, there are people in our lives who do care about us. But if you ask yourself what it is that *you* want for the people you love, I believe that your answer will be rather simple: we want our loved ones to be happy. We might want them to be successful, healthy, and financially stable, and we have our own ideas about achieving these goals, but ultimately, we just want them to be happy.

So the world doesn't need your perfection—it is an illusion. The best gift you can give to the world is your happiness. So let's talk about it.

I'm not sure of your background and upbringing, but I was brought up on classical literature, particularly of the 19th century European authors, with their high ideals and strict morals. Add to this an idealistic Soviet society, where grand schemes of future universal happiness were more important than the life of a single individual, and you will get someone with a serious martyr complex.[31]

A lot of us justly believe that it is noble to sacrifice yourself to something much bigger and more important than your own life. And it is—in the right place and the right time, but not always.

When the Soviet Union was still standing strong, Estonian activists started a campaign for the independence of our little country. They gathered signatures of ordinary people to support the proclamation of independence. If you wonder if that was something safe to do, then the answer is absolutely *not*! We are talking about a country where people were imprisoned, jailed, and killed for not only thinking differently, but for merely "owning too much."[32]

We are talking about a country where my father's career was stunted because he had relatives who lived abroad and because he was not a member of the Communist party. So when my mother gave a signature for the independence of Estonia, she was warned that she was doing something very dangerous and that her party membership would be revoked. This was an act of putting a grand idea above your own individual safety. But that grand idea led to a revolution, an independence of an occupied country, a change of regime. Later, my mother was granted Estonian citizenship for her loyalty (since she was a migrant into the country and didn't qualify to be granted the citizenship jus sanguinis).

There will be situations where you have to be courageous and possibly disregard your own personal interests and safety. But such situations do not happen often unless you work in rescue services and save lives on a daily basis. For most of us regular people, such situations *never* come to pass. I have experienced one big revolution in my life—the downfall of the USSR. But the next "big thing" that happened to me was 30 years later in February 2022—the war on my own doorstep, when Russia attacked Ukraine, unprovoked and extremely brutally.

Yet most of us keep being martyrs and sacrificing our own happiness for some ephemeral grand ideas on a daily basis. We stay in jobs we hate (sacrifice) because we need to pay bills (grand idea). We stay in relationships that don't work (sacrifice) for the sake of our children (grand idea). We compromise our happiness (sacrifice) for the sake of not upsetting someone else (grand idea).

While there is time and place to be a hero, I want you to recognise that most of the time, we compromise our own happiness for the sake of avoiding a conflict, not rocking the boat, preserving the status quo, keeping up good appearances, and all such nonsense.

And you might argue at this point, "Surely there are things in life (that may not be as extreme as a revolution) that are more important than your own happiness?"

Before I got into business, I used to work in nonprofits and charities. I have done it on all possible levels—local charities, global nonprofits, intergovernmental organisations—and have even done charity on my own initiative, with my own funding on a grassroots level. In the early 2000s, when my company, Mindvalley, was still young, I was deeply involved in work with refugees in Malaysia. I was working for United Nations High Commissioner for

Refugees (UNHCR) with communities from Myanmar. The stories of the people that I worked with were horrendous. A lot of them had lost everything: their families and loved ones, their possessions and homes. Even if their lives in Malaysia were better than what they had fled from, they were still far from "well" and definitely not safe. So, naturally, I was exposed to a lot of human suffering on a daily basis, and my instinct was to try and help everyone I met.

At the same time, we were building Mindvalley—a company that is still helping people to live happy, fulfilled, extraordinary lives to this day. And now my favourite birdie—cognitive dissonance—was a natural outcome of my two worlds clashing.

Once I had a chance to attend a small gathering with His Holiness the Dalai Lama, and I couldn't help asking him what to do—how could I think about happiness and fulfilment when there was so much suffering in the world? Dalai Lama's answer to me was simple, but it stuck forever:

"Kristina, you cannot help anyone if you are not happy."

You cannot help anyone if you are not happy.

You may fool yourself into believing that you are sacrificing your happiness for the sake of people that you love, but it is a lie. You can fool yourself, but you will not fool your loved ones—your children, your loving intuitive mother, or your partner who might be able to decipher your mood from the way you breathe.

The people that you love do not need your sacrifice—they need you to be happy. So not only is your sacrifice of personal happiness pointless, but it is also a heavy burden on those for whom you so selflessly want to make the offering.

Reflection Points

What does *happiness* mean to you? How would one day of your happy life look? I want you to write a short essay on the topic "A Perfect Day." Here are the rules:

- Imagine a perfect day in your happy life. Pick a regular weekday, when you do your job or your calling. Start in the morning—you wake up, move through the day. Imagine doing your work, meeting your peers, then move on to the evening, spending time with your loved ones, and finish at night. What do you think or feel when you go to bed?

- Describe your perfect day, unrestricted by your current circumstances, responsibilities, and limitations. Write it like a movie script—anything is possible.

- Try to write quickly without overthinking or criticising. Play. Have fun!

- This is not a goal-setting exercise, so you don't need to know how and when you are going to make this day a reality. The point of this exercise is to understand what makes you truly happy.

A POINTLESS
Sacrifice

*Self-sacrifice enables us to sacrifice
other people without blushing.*

— G. BERNARD SHAW[33]

When I started my first independent business in 2003, I had a partner. When we started our business together, Ivy[34] and I had a lot in common—both newbies, both brave and a little reckless, both young mothers. Even our children became friends. And since we were also both little Hermiones, we did well—we grew our business to the first million dollars in the first few years and were immensely pleased with ourselves. But that's where the goodness ended.

Sometime at the height of our success and growing friendship, doubt crept into my heart. I started noticing red flags—we had different business mentalities, and our approaches could not be more contradictory. Yet contradiction was what we both tried to avoid. I don't know about my partner, but on my part, I can say that I was terrified of contradiction and conflict. So we chose to compromise—not the best choice for business success, since compromise is often the epitome of indecision.

Things were similarly turbulent in our personal relationship. I felt, or feared, that my partner was dissatisfied with our friendship and that feeling was growing day by day in conviction and intensity. I remember one morning taking a shower before work and dreading the moment

I had to step foot in the office and face her. I started wondering—Is this right? Should I be going on like this if I feel miserable every working day?

But I pushed that doubt aside because the Good Girl in me was convinced that the right thing to do was to keep going, despite my worry, despite my own unhappiness, to safeguard her feelings. If you are an entrepreneur, like me, you might have caught yourself feeling something similar at some point in your business: as the founder, you have to set aside your personal feelings and keep going for the sake of everyone else.

And that was the beautiful story I started telling myself: "Kristina, you have to keep going for the sake of your employees, your customers, your partners, for the sake of this grand idea." I decided that pushing aside my own unhappiness and grinding on was not only something a real entrepreneur would do, but it was my moral duty for the sake of the betterment of humanity.

Such a pile of nonsense!

I was feeding myself that story for three long years, when I could have cut it all loose and counted my losses much sooner. When my relationship with Ivy came to the point of being unbearable, I decided I couldn't go on lying to myself. There was no grand idea nor necessary sacrifice for the greater good, there was just my fear to be in business alone, to take on full responsibility and all of the risks on my own two shoulders. I was avoiding the loss of my crutch: this dysfunctional partnership. I was simply scared.

I did, finally, summon the courage to propose splitting up with my partner. And what followed was messy, painful, and a little unsavoury. But not only did I survive on my own, I thrived. I remember the morning after I proposed the separation. I was standing in my bathroom, looking at my reflection in the mirror, and I felt light and happy. I felt like I had wings behind my back.

So was my sacrifice necessary? I endured being miserable for three years for the sake of my employees, customers, and partners. Yet none of them needed it. A few years after our separation, an employee of mine (who had been with me from the very start, through the glory and the pain, through the separation with Ivy to my own solo journey) told me: "Kristina, you were keeping up appearances with Ivy and trying so hard to keep it normal for all of us, but we knew how unhappy you two were. It was so painful to work with you. You cannot imagine how much lighter and happier I feel now that you have finally found peace with yourself and your business."

I sacrificed myself for my team—but my sacrifice turned out to be a heavy burden for both myself *and* them.

In summary, the world doesn't need your sacrifice. The world doesn't need your perfection. What the world needs is for you to be yourself—and, of course, for you to be happy.

Reflection Points

This is another introspection exercise. Think of a situation in your life where you are sacrificing your own well-being for someone else, or placing a grand idea above your own happiness. Maybe you love helping people and you do that to your own detriment. Maybe you stay in a relationship to avoid a conflict. Maybe you are in a wrong job because you cannot let down your family and risk a steady income.

- Why are you choosing to sacrifice your well-being in this situation?

- How does this sacrifice make you feel?

- What would be an ideal solution to this uncomfortable situation?

- If you had courage to say no in this situation, how would it make you feel?

DODGING *Impostor* SYNDROME

We ask ourselves, "Who am I to be brilliant, gorgeous, talented, fabulous?" Actually, who are you not to be? You are a child of God. Your playing small does not serve the world. There is nothing enlightened about shrinking so that other people won't feel insecure around you. We are all meant to shine, as children do. We were born to make manifest the glory of God that is within us. It's not just in some of us; it's in everyone. And as we let our own light shine, we unconsciously give other people permission to do the same.

— MARIANNE WILLIAMSON[35]

And the question is—are you ready to be your true self? Are you ready to live a fulfilled life by your own rules?

I know I wasn't.

I remember standing on the big stage of our flagship event, A-Fest, my first time as an author and a transformational teacher (I'd recently launched my first online course), ready to speak about my own framework for happiness. A great personal achievement, no doubt, but how do you think I felt at that moment?

Accomplished? Proud? Happy?

Far from it! I felt like a fraud.

"Who am I to stand on this stage and teach anyone?" I had just heard some of the best speakers in the world make their presentations. Who was I to follow in their footsteps? I didn't have the same energy and explosive conviction as speaker A. I didn't have the same accomplishments and success to back up my message as speakers B and C. And I didn't even have a best-selling book like speaker D did. What did I have to offer?

Comparison is a slippery road. No matter how much you do, how high you climb, or what you accomplish, there is always someone who has done more, climbed higher, and has more impressive achievements.

In his book *Love Yourself Like Your Life Depends on It*, Kamal Ravikant,[36] a successful Silicon Valley investor and a great inspiration to me personally, shares his own story of comparison. Even someone like Kamal started out comparing himself to other successful entrepreneurs and investors. And this led him into a dark depression with suicidal thoughts.

When I was standing on my first big stage, wondering how I ended up there and who I thought I was, I continued comparing myself on a loop, facet by painful facet:

- Presentation skills? There's someone better.
- Business success? There are so many who are more successful.
- I haven't written a book yet? Well, most speakers have.
- I have a few years of experience? Well, most of the world-famous people have clocked up decades.

But if you take yourself into pieces and tear yourself down piece by piece, there will be nothing left. Nothing to improve, nothing to grow, nothing to compare.

Fast forward a few years, and I am again on my next biggest stage with the most incredible lineup of speakers.

And again, I'm nervous and feeling like a fraud. In the run-up to my speech, I was hiding from people around the corner of the conference hall. There were hardly any passersby, but one woman stopped and exclaimed: "Oh my God! It is you! I cannot wait to hear you. You are so real, so relatable. When you speak, I almost feel like you are talking to me personally."

I never asked that woman her name, but her passing remark became a turning point in my career. I realised that what she valued in me was *me*—the real me, with my flaws and insecurities, with my relatability and vulnerability. My value was not in my accomplishments, but in my unique mix of what made me the person that I am.

On that big and intimidating stage, I was standing, the little girl inside me scared and breathless, but confident, nevertheless, because I'd chosen to believe that the world needed me and my message. It didn't need another replica of a famous and accomplished speaker, it didn't need a copycat of a best-selling author, it didn't need the Perfect Girl that I liked to pretend to be—it needed *me*, with all my flaws, dents, scratches, and insecurities, and with all my beautiful dragons. The world needed my flawesome self.

What makes you valuable is not that you might be the best in the world at something. What makes you valuable is your unique mix of experiences, expertise, failings, and mistakes.

So, are you ready to embrace yourself the way you are? Because I swear, it will be the best gift you could ever give to the world.

Reflection Points

Let's meditate on the idea of being *flawesome*. Literally, let's do a little self-guided meditation. Here's how it works:

- Sit comfortably, close your eyes, take a deep breath, feel your body. Relax physically. Feel how your body is relaxed.

- Now answer this question: What kind of person would I be if I were flawesome?

- If I was at peace with my flaws and imperfections, with my dragons, how would I feel? What would I be able to do? How would I dare to challenge myself?

- If I could do what I truly love doing, what I am good at, what kind of person would that make me? How would I feel about it? How would I dare to challenge myself?

- Take another deep breath, relax, stay in this feeling. When you open your eyes, you can write down your thoughts, feelings, and realisations in your journal.

PART V

Honesty

PARADIGM SHIFT
STARTS WITH A
Decision

It's been my experience that you can nearly always enjoy things if you make up your mind firmly that you will.

— LUCY MAUD MONTGOMERY[1]

It's time to go deep. Enough prep work and pep talks.

You can live authentically, sincerely, and unapologetically. You can embrace your flawesomeness and love yourself unconditionally. It is all accessible to you right now, without any further delays.

All it takes is a decision and, just like Bilbo Baggins, you will set off on your journey and you will never be the same old hobbit again.

Living in your truth and embracing your flawesomeness does not require an effort on your part; it doesn't require following certain routines or establishing new practises. People are naturally drawn to simple ritualistic solutions. But changes don't happen like that. I wish there were a recipe, a clear tutorial, a simple hack, a magic pill, but there are none.

Often, when people want to bring about a change, they put in more effort, try a little harder, study a little deeper. But change doesn't happen because you *want* it to happen—it happens when you are ready for it. One day, seemingly out of nowhere, everything just clicks into place, and Bam! your life has changed.

My very first personal growth training, which I attended as a regular participant (not in work capacity), took place in 2008. It was a four-day intensive training and I had just become a mother, so I took my baby with me. I was nursing Hayden between the sessions and at night, only to wake up early in the morning and go for a long day of intense and physically demanding training.

I hated the experience (and the people)! But then, such arrogance and cynicism were quite normal for me at that time in my life. I had just moved to Malaysia after living in New York and studying in Edinburgh, and I felt anything but ready to settle in Asia. Every time I had to go to renew my visa in the immigration department, I would secretly hope that my visa would get rejected, and I could have a valid reason to escape back to Europe.

I lived in my bubble of reality, or should I say, my own version of reality, my parallel universe, and I was blissfully content with the way I saw the world. The only (minor) problem was that I did not like where I was, and I wanted to escape.

Escape to where? Good question! I didn't really know or care. All I knew was that I didn't want to be where I was—in Malaysia.

It was sometime between days two and three of the personal growth event when I had a strange lightbulb moment. A thought descended on me, out of nowhere, with no connection to the actual training: "Hayden is growing up, and he will go to school one day, probably here, in Malaysia. So, it seems that Malaysia is my home now, whether I like it or not. Isn't it wiser to like it, rather than not?"

Just like that, in the middle of chaos, I decided to like everything I disliked so passionately a few moments earlier. I decided to like Malaysia, to like my life in my new home, and to like whatever was going on with me and my body at that time.

The training was actually great in the end, by the way. I still think it was one of the best personal growth training sessions I have ever attended. It was absolutely brilliant, and I was lucky to have my paradigm shift[2] in time to enjoy the last two days.

And my life turned around 180 degrees: where things used to be awful, they became awesome and with no effort on my part. I finally fully immersed myself into Asian life, going wholeheartedly after everything it had to offer and seeking joy and pleasure in the experiences, rather than reluctantly dragging myself along as I used to do before. It wasn't an effort or a constant struggle. I just made a decision—it was that simple!

This simple experience was one of the most profound transformative moments in my life. It definitely made a great difference in the quality of my life. But more than that, it gave me a chance to experience a crucial concept in personal growth—that your perception defines your reality.

The moment your perception changes, or your paradigm shifts, your life starts changing, adjusting to the new paradigm.

And I want to be very clear—by no means am I talking about the law of attraction or any other such simplified occult ideas. It is a paradigm shift that we are chasing, a profound change in the way you view and understand reality.

Paradigm shifts cannot be thought up, intellectualised, or rationalised—they just have to be experienced. Do you remember my formula for transformation? Knowledge + experience = transformation. Experience alone will not necessarily transform you; it requires the right kind of context to give you the transformation. Yet, mere knowledge without experience is like a dusty book on a shelf—it will change nothing in your life, unless you validate the knowledge with your own experience.

So don't let this book gather dust, both literally and figuratively speaking. You have to translate ideas from this book into experiences. And to facilitate such experiences, you will need a few vital skills: courage, honesty, and kindness.

I do not pretend that these skills are new for you, but let's shift them into the focus of your attention. We'll start with honesty because it is that quality that sets the wheels in motion. Then we'll talk about kindness, because without it, honesty can cause more damage than good. And finally, we'll talk about courage—the skill that you will need at every step of the way, but more so when you start taking action to change your life as a result of mastering honesty and kindness.

Reflection Points

You are more than halfway through, and if you have come this far, you must have had your share of discoveries, realisations, and maybe even a paradigm shift. At this point, what will be beneficial for you is to pause for a moment and let your thoughts and feelings settle. The best way to do it is to take out your trusty journal and answer this question (in writing):

- What have been my biggest discoveries and realisations so far?

Just put it all down on paper, and after you are done, go for another solo walk without gadgets or distractions. Spend some quality time with yourself.

LET'S BE HONEST ABOUT
Honesty

To believe all men honest would be folly.
To believe none so is something worse.

— JOHN QUINCY ADAMS[3]

Do you remember the once hugely popular TV series *Lie to Me*?

There was a secondary character in the show, Eli Loker, who was practising radical honesty.[4] He openly vocalised everything that came to his mind, without filters or considering social context or feelings of others. This is not the kind of honesty I want you to practise (thank god!).

Actually, I was taken aback by the idea of radical honesty. Coupled with the show's main message that everyone at all times is trying to hide something and the fantastic notion that you can easily read other people's innermost feelings just by noticing their micro-expressions, it would be quite accurate to say that I had a complicated relationship with honesty.

How much honesty is the right amount? Mostly honest? One hundred percent honest? Where do you draw the line between honesty and bad manners? And where do you draw the line between withholding honesty and giving yourself space to process emotions? Finally, is an absence of honesty invariably the same as deception?

By nature, I am a rather reserved person. People are often misguided by my image of authenticity, equating authenticity to absolute honesty, but this is an erroneous idea. I may talk openly about certain experiences in my life and some of my personal feelings, and I admit my mistakes and unpleasant emotions rather easily, but there are areas which I prefer to keep private, especially love, romantic relationships, and sex. Furthermore, intense emotional experiences, which I am in the process of digesting, are not something I am ready to discuss publicly. So, there are plenty of areas that I'd like to keep private.

And so, the question of public honesty (as opposed to personal) was something I needed to ponder. Drawing a line between public and private was imperative for me. I was not ready to start a discussion on honesty unless I could be sure that I could keep my privacy where it most mattered to me.

There are a few important and sensitive points that we have to discuss before we dive into honesty. The topic might sound innocent on the surface, but to discuss honesty in depth, we will have to touch upon its more controversial opposites: lying and deceit.

Here I need to make a serious disclaimer. When we touch upon the topics of lying and deceit, I am only talking about "milder" forms of such behaviour, if there is at all a possibility of drawing a line between okay-lying and not-okay-lying. And you may object at this point that no lying is ever okay, but give me a few minutes, and I will show you that lying is not as simple a phenomenon as it might seem.

For me to be able to talk about lying and deceit in a clinical sort of way, I need your dispassionate attention, which in the case of lying might not be so easily attainable. Starting with mainstream religions and ancient philosophers, through classical literature and contemporary popular culture, we are indoctrinated to vilify any form of deception. Deception is invariably considered immoral and often linked to criminal intent.

And so, I would like to make a distinction between antisocial (in extreme cases) and criminal sorts of deception and "milder," more casual deceptions. If we look deeper into deception, we'll see that it is not a binary phenomenon, but rather a scale with various degrees of severity, with nonmalicious and often unintended deceit on the opposite end from criminal lying.

Another disclaimer that I need to make is a caution against a new batch of buzzwords. This, I'm sure, does not come as a surprise, but such words as *honesty, truth, lying,* and *deceit* come with hefty baggage, sensitive moral and ethical implications, and strong emotional biases. As before, I'm asking you to erase the buzz (if you can) and look at these phenomena as natural biological functions of mammals with highly evolved brains.[5]

Questioning truth or claiming that deception is a natural behaviour in humans will bring upon me some accusations of immorality or lack of ethical ideals, but I assure you that I am not a moral relativist. I may be a little relativist when it comes to truth, but I am not questioning honesty, or morality for that matter.

What I would like to achieve is to challenge this curious juxtaposition of honesty and deceit, and rather than see them as polar opposites, understand that they are closely connected, forming a complete and whole entity, like yin and yang. It is imperative to understand both clearly, without biases.

Finally, I am by far more interested in the personal expression of these phenomena. In the chart below, I placed honesty and deceit on scale X, and their public versus private expression on scale Y. My interest is primarily in the lower quarters of the chart. Public expressions of both honesty and deceit are important in general, but less so in the context of finding your way back to yourself.

This book is about your relationship with the self, and in this topic, just as before, the rule holds: your relationship with the world is a mirror reflection of your relationship with yourself. Once you fix your relationship with yourself (lower quarters on the chart), your relationship with the world will fall into place (upper quarters on the chart).

Outward and inward expression of honesty and deceit

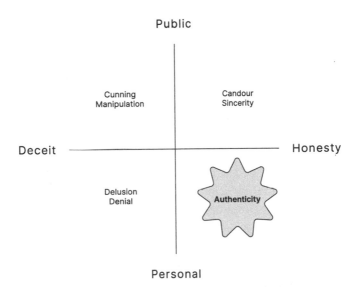

Reflection Points

Remember, you are doing this exercise for yourself. I am not going to check on you, and you will not need to show your results to anyone. Ready?

- Rate your self-honesty on a scale of 0 to 10, where 0 is "I lie to myself all the time" and 10 is "I am radically and uncompromisingly honest with myself."

$\mathscr{Self}$-HONESTY

Living a more honest life starts with confronting our own deception, instead of simply noticing everyone else's.

— JUDI KETTELER[6]

When I am on stage delivering my talk on authenticity, I often ask people to rate their self-honesty; in other words, how honest they think they are with themselves.

It's a safe question, because lying to yourself is not considered a vice; rather it is more like a personal misfortune. So, there would be no harm in honestly admitting that once in a while you tell yourself a beautiful fairy tale, and then sincerely believe in it.

There would be no harm in admitting self-deception, so how do you think people reply to my question? Well, from what I can see on stage, the answers are predominantly in favour of self-honesty. People sincerely believe that they are honest with themselves.

As I explained in the previous chapter, I'm not going to be too hard on you regarding lying to the world. It is self-deception that interests me the most. Because how can we be truly honest if we are in the dark about the lies that we tell ourselves? And the most absurd part about self-deception is that we are, by definition, unaware of being delusional.

I hate to share unfashionable news, but deception is human nature.

And what may be even more surprising is that lying is woven into the fabric of social interaction. According to researcher Pamela Meyer, we are lied to from 10 to 200 times a day.[7] (Actually, the estimates of average casual lies we are exposed to on a daily basis are a bit confusing, ranging from 1.65 into several hundred. But I wouldn't obsess about the exact number.)

It may initially look like an overestimation, but think of all the acceptable forms of lying that we are often exposed to. The white lies that are told for the benefit of others and in some cases, for example in medical practise, may be lifesaving. Or the rules of civility, which prescribe pleasant answers to greetings or questions such as: "Do you like this cake?" rather than an honest response. Or lying by omission: when information is simply withheld, such situations are very hard to confront because there is no way to confirm if the omission was made intentionally. The point is, as bad a vice as we consider lying to be, it is prevalently practised in our daily lives.

But let's look at lies clinically, as I promised earlier. Lying and deception are a natural quality of our brain's functioning. Children start lying almost as early as they learn to talk. By the age of five, most children are quite comfortable with the concept of lying and start experimenting with misrepresenting reality to their advantage. With age, children learn to lie more believably and maintain their lies better.

I should say that this is the case for most children, but not all. My eldest child, Hayden, was diagnosed with high-functioning Asperger's syndrome at the age of six. His school was very supportive and sent me for professional training on this condition, which I found both very helpful and incredibly interesting. To my great surprise, I found out that children with Asperger's syndrome have difficulty lying. It is a skill that doesn't come naturally to such kids.

The reason for this is interesting: lying and deception require advanced cognitive and executive functions, such as understanding the theory of mind, being good at perspective taking, and consequently, having developed empathy—these are not the fortes of kids with Asperger's.

In addition to empathy and understanding complicated cognitive concepts, lying requires memory and ability to maintain parallel versions of reality simultaneously. In other words, it is no surprise that lying is considered a milestone in a child's development. In fact, some scientists point out that lying and creativity employ essentially the same cognitive skills.[8]

It turns out that lying is a skill that requires advanced brain functioning. But not just that, lying requires more effort than being honest.[9] That is not surprising, of course, and part of the reason why lying fires up more of your brain is because making a decision about lying, a moral dilemma that you have to resolve, takes up additional effort.

"Why does it matter?" you might ask. Lying requires additional mental work, yet our brain works on a "minimal required effort" regime—our brain is geared to find paths that require the least mental strain.[10] It would make sense to conclude that humans must have very compelling reasons to lie, since it is not the path of least resistance. And we do, for a variety of reasons, but most importantly, we lie to bridge the gap between reality and how we would actually like it to be.

I will not go into all the reasons why people lie to each other, since that would be a completely different book, but I would, however, like to focus on *why* we lie to ourselves, and *why* we are dishonest about not being honest.

The reason why we are dishonest with ourselves is, again, yes, clinical. Our brain is a great illusionist with just one function—to save and protect us from harm, or death, to be precise. And since rejection, as we have already established, from the point of view of our brain is, literally, a question of life and death, then appearing good is rather high on our brain's priority list.

And so, with such a noble cause as saving us from harm, our brain is hard at work, not just looking out for danger and sending us warning signals, but also creating a safe version of reality for us to reside in. Our brain is like an overbearing parent who wants their child to be safe at any cost. Or a slightly creepier analogy is that it is like our own personal matrix keeping us content and unaware.

In short, your brain doesn't like gaps, chaos, or uncertainty, so it fills the gaps with imagination and presents it as reality. There are many curious phenomena that prove that your brain is hard at work tricking you, such as various cognitive biases, which distort your perception of real events.[11] Or the tendency to use mental shortcuts[12] while making a decision and then seeking out proof of being right the moment the decision has been made.[13] And I could go on and on with a list of tricks that your brain uses on you: optical illusions, inattentional blindness, phantom pains, placebo, just to mention a few familiar ones. And, of course, any kind of illusions and biases, even if you are blissfully unaware of being tricked, can distort your perception of reality.

So it would be right to say that self-deception is not you lying to yourself, but your brain tricking you into viewing the world in a way that is most beneficial to you.

Another example of self-deception are defence mechanisms—denial, distortion, reaction formation, and the rest of the gang, which we discussed in Part IV. This kind of lying to self happens unconsciously as well.

Most of us are much more comfortable with deception than we might like to admit. And just like with self-deception, we are often rather comfortable with being lied to or twisting the truth when presenting our case to others. Unfortunately, some of such deception is hard to catch and almost impossible to avoid completely.

Honesty starts with being honest about lying. If you can admit that sometimes you lie to yourself (and sometimes to others), then you are ready to ask yourself this uncomfortable question:

"Is this the truth, or is this the story I'd like to believe in?"

And that brings us to the next important concept: the truth.

Reflection Points

This is yet another twist to our (now) favourite awareness exercise from Part III of this book. Anchor your moments of awareness to situations when you are telling yourself a story. Maybe you made a blunder, and you are giving yourself an explanation. Maybe you are "rehearsing" recent events in your head. Maybe you had a hard conversation or a conflict and you keep "arguing" with your opponent in your own mind.

When you catch yourself telling yourself another story, pause for a moment and ask:

- Is this the truth, or is this the story I'd like to believe?

THERE IS NO
Spoon

*A rock pile ceases to be a rock pile the moment
a single man contemplates it, bearing within
him the image of a cathedral.*

— ANTOINE DE SAINT-EXUPÉRY[14]

I was very nervous to meet my friend, Dmitry Shamenkov, for the first time. He is a medical doctor, an author and a speaker, and the creator of the Open Dialogue method— one of the deepest and most profound transformative teachings, in my opinion. I have learned an incredible amount from Dmitry and his method, but that came later. First, I was afraid.

Dmitry teaches Open Dialogue, and simply put, it is all about complete honesty. I remember when we had set up a dinner date to be introduced, I felt concerned, wondering if I would have to share some deep private secrets with Dmitry and if I was expected to attend his "honesty training."

I met Dmitry at a time when I was going through painful and confusing transformative experiences, those which I was not yet ready to spill out for everyone's information. And so, I went to meet with my now-very-dear friend in a state of trepidation, as if I were going for a police interrogation. Needless to say, we had a thoroughly enjoyable dinner, and Dmitry seemed to me like some kind of wise and flawless otherworldly creature. That dinner marked the beginning of my journey toward honesty. Because honesty is a sharp weapon, and you have to learn to use it properly before you start wielding it.

In our Western, somewhat dogmatic culture, the attitude to truth is a little uptight and testy. As one of my social media followers put it: "Can we live as rational beings with absolute truth? Or is that an out-of-reach ideal?"

This "absolute truth" concept is classic—it fully expresses our idealistic and dogmatic approach to truth. But is truth really such a straightforward concept?[15] What is absolute truth anyway? In fact, it may be dangerous to stay true to what you deem to be absolute truth. After all, there is a possibility that we only ever have a version of "truth" seen through unique lenses.

Steve Jobs famously said: "Don't be trapped by dogma—which is living with the results of other people's thinking."[16] While Jobs was referring to other people's thoughts and opinions, I'd like to expand this brilliant idea—the world that we inhabit now was created by humans based on our understanding of reality. We came up with the rules, and then we followed those made-up rules and created a reality, which, predictably, proved our made-up rules to be "true." And then we have the audacity to claim that our made-up rules are universal, that they are the rules of nature, in fact, and prove the point with the observation that our made-up world functions on such rules.[17]

Some philosophers, of course, have pronounced that there are also universal rules of morality, similar to the universal rules of nature, and questioning the idea of absolute truth is relativist. I will not argue, because I am relativist when it comes to defining truth, but I want to drive a point forward: questioning absolute truth doesn't mean that one has to reject morality or honesty.

In his online course, Vishen Lakhiani introduces a great, practical concept of distinguishing between absolute and relative truths.[18] *Absolute truth* is what is true for everyone regardless of parameters or context, while *relative truth* is true for one person, but might not be true for everyone. My main thesis is that hardly any of our human truths are absolutes, except perhaps the laws of nature as defined by physicists.

- To say that Earth is a huge rock flying through space at a great speed, based on our current understanding of physics, is an absolute truth, even if flat-earthers might be rejecting the idea. But the thought that Earth's gravitational force cannot be defied might have been absolute truth for generations, until humans conquered space travel (and it turned out to be a relative truth).

- It is quite safe to say that ageing is an absolute concept: with time, everyone ages. But to equate ageing with loss of health, fitness, and energy is not quite so absolute anymore. We live in the age of agelessness, and we see countless examples of people who defy the traditional concepts of old age. For them, loss of health, fitness, and energy is a relative truth that they prefer to reject.

- You might say that the idea that hard work brings success is an absolute truth because most of the world lives by that rule, but in my personal opinion, it is but a relative truth by which many people choose to live and function, and so it manifests in their reality.

A lot of truths may seem absolute to us because we were brought up in this paradigm and kept seeing proof of such ideas in our daily reality: people lose health with age, people work hard to become successful, etc. But if you remember our discussion on the reticular activating system, then you will not wonder why you see proof of those truths, which inhabit your current paradigm.

People keep defying absolute truths and opening up the limits of reality. And at times, you might be proven wrong, or right, it does not matter, as long as you keep pushing the boundaries of what's possible—which is why I decided that I'm done ageing. It might sound funny or strange, and I might turn out to be wrong and look like a baked apple when I'm 100, but I have nothing to lose, except the infirmity of old age.

This chapter, however, is not about what's possible; it's about a proverbial spoon,[19] which doesn't really exist. It is only your mind that bends around it.

"But there are moral and ethical questions and simply the truth of hard facts," you might say. And you are right—there are social norms, morality, and ethics, and even empathy and compassion, which all have a claim on defining absolute truths. But I do invite you to look at all truths presented to you with a simple question in mind: "Is it absolute or relative?"

I suspect that if you dig deep enough, few truths will ever prove to be absolute. Humankind has rejected so many of its old beliefs, and we keep reinventing every area of life over and over again—nutrition, fitness, health, love, relationships, parenthood—what was the truth 50 years ago is now often considered outdated and obsolete.

In short, questioning absolutes is not the same as rejecting social norms, rules, ethics, or morality. I'm rather inviting you to embark on an internal process of reevaluating your own beliefs and paradigms.

Now, if most truth is relative and hardly any truth is absolute, then it is logical to assume that even the truth that you have chosen to adopt—Your Truth—no matter why you chose to adopt it, might be relative. And this is an important point—even Your Truth, the truth that you chose to adopt for yourself, is only just that—*your* Truth.

The next very important step toward honesty is accepting this simple axiom: you might be wrong.

That very simple exercise will let you off the hook of your own ego, of your bulletproof delusion, and open you up to real honesty with yourself. Because, whether you like it or not, we lie to ourselves the most, often unwittingly and unintentionally, but we do.

Reflection Points

I invite you to do a very simple exercise. In the next few days, every time you hear a generalising statement about how something works, whether it is success, happiness, life, money, health, or love, ask yourself these two simple questions:

- Is It absolute truth, or might it be relative?
- Can I think of any examples or any people who defy this generally accepted truth?

FAKING IT

Some people fake their death, I'm faking my life.

— DON DELILLO[20]

Do you remember the conversation about perfectionism in the very beginning of our journey? As with all evil doings, the road to self-deception is paved with good intentions.

Of course, you want to be a Good Girl or a Good Boy. Of course, you have a picture of perfection in your mind. Of course, you do everything to match your reality with that imaginary picture. We are told to "fake it till we make it," and while I understand the logic of that saying, I think it causes more harm than good, because it sets us off on the path of self-deception.

You cannot take "faking" in this expression too literally because:

- There is a difference between doing your best and being righteous.

- There is a difference between having courage to take action and overpromising.

- There is a difference between the mindset of abundance and spending recklessly.

- There is a difference between believing in your message and claiming that you know the truth.

- There is a difference between feeling content and forcing "good vibes only."

- There is a difference between a paradigm shift
  and half-hearted affirmations.

I am for courage, action, good faith, and giving it your best, but I have serious reservations against faking of any kind—pretending, acting the part, mindlessly following rituals, or turning a blind eye to the obvious. I wholeheartedly agree that if you want different results in your life, you need to do something different—but if you want a profound change, you have to see into the essence of phenomena; you have to go beyond the facade, beyond the faking.

Any personal growth and transformation practise will work only as well, as profoundly you understand and accept the ritual involved. Your self-talk has to be believable; your actions have to be coherent with your worldview. But more importantly, you cannot fake a belief.

If you don't think that earning money is easy, no amount of convincing yourself that "the Universe is abundant" will change how you feel about money. If you don't love the current version of yourself, no amount of chanting that "you are lovable as you are" will change how you really feel about yourself. If you don't believe in your talent, no amount of faking will change how you perceive your own value.

Sometimes rituals do help you make a shift, and the beauty of such practises is that they are meant to work like a magic pill. But they depend on faking and self-deception, at least initially, and that is never a good start of a relationship.

Real change happens when you have the courage to dive deep, to see the essence of things, to be honest, even brutally honest with yourself, and accept reality as it is. When you can see the world differently because your view has changed, and not because you would like to see it differently. When you can actually feel the joy in the present moment, and not just put on rose-tinted glasses. When you can love yourself with your flaws and not just hope that you are lovable despite being imperfect.

There is a huge, massive, insurmountable difference between faking your way into a new life and actually seeing the world in the new light.

I started my path into personal growth with all the traditional trainings and teachings, and I, too, have tried to fake it. I had been faking it for 40 years, and I was very convincing—until I realised that I was tired of faking it. I wanted the real thing.

The path to "the real thing" lies through complete and unreserved honesty. And that is what I will talk about next.

Reflection Points

Take a moment for introspection. Are there any areas in your life where you might be "faking it"? Maybe you have challenged yourself beyond your capabilities. Maybe you have overspent hoping to attract more abundance. Maybe you are ignoring your true feelings in an attempt to be liked or accepted. Maybe you are trying too hard hoping to save a turbulent relationship.

Ask yourself are you *faking* it, or are you giving it *your best*? Can you feel the difference between the two?

USING HONESTY
Safely

*Suppose that we were able to share meanings freely
without a compulsive urge to impose our view or to conform
to those of others and without distortion and self-deception.
Would this not constitute a real revolution in culture
and therefore eventually in society?*

— DAVID BOHM[21]

My friend Dmitry Shamenkov created what I believe to be one of the deepest and most profound, transformative teachings. The Open Dialogue technique is all about complete honesty. Dmitri came up with a set of principles to facilitate a natural discussion in small groups. People come together, agree on the rules, and then have an hour-long discussion.

The rules for Open Dialogue are very deep and profound, but they're simple too—so simple, in fact, that I started using them as a framework for my everyday life.

It was those very rules and principles that opened me up to real, courageous, and compassionate honesty with myself and the world. So, with little alterations to account for a different context, I've decided to adopt them as rules, or rather instructions, for communicating with honesty.

1. Clarity—about the goal;
2. Acceptance—everyone has the right to be themselves;
3. Nonviolence—no teaching, preaching, fixing, or judging;

4. No stories—it is about your present emotions;

5. Sincerity;

6. Personal practise.

And now, let's dive deeper into each of the rules separately.

1. CLARITY

A journey begins once you set a destination. Having a destination is equally important in any human interaction. What is the goal of your interaction? What is the destination? And rule number one in Open Dialogue is being clear about your goal.

If you remember the part about the reticular activating system, you might remember the simple conclusion our little experiment drove us to—your goal defines your perception. If you are set on noticing a certain colour, that colour is what you will see in your environment. By this analogy:

- if you are set to solve a disagreement, your brain will focus on picking up clues toward a solution;

- if you are set on discovering common truth, your brain will focus on that task;

- if you are set on proving your opponent wrong, your brain will show you how your opponent is wrong and you are right; and

- if you are set on fixing your partner, your brain will feed this aspiration with all the signs of your partner's vast improvability.

This principle seems clear enough on paper, but think of the last time you had an argument or a heated discussion with someone—how conscious were you of the goal of your interaction?

We often rush into a verbal fight thinking that we are out there for the truth, but without making a conscious pause to think and reflect about the actual goals of an interaction, our trickster brain takes over and supplies us with the easiest and often unconscious goal—to prove that you are right. And this is not the same as discovering a common truth, or coming to an agreement, or understanding your partner's point of view, or hearing what's in their heart, or improving the depth and warmth of your connection.

In arguments, we often feel threatened, even attacked, and we put on the defence mode and start fighting our corner. Yet, in the previous few chapters, we came to two very distressing conclusions: we have a tendency toward self-deception and our truth might not be absolute. With these two points in mind, the goal of wanting to be right just doesn't seem like the best aspiration.

And so, rule number one is: be clear about your goal.

2. ACCEPTANCE

Every time you want to be right, there is a collateral aspiration to change your opponent's point of view. In essence, it is a desire to change another person. When you are contradicted, you don't usually question your position, you question your opponent. "Why can't they see my point? What is wrong with them?"

Let's take obvious examples—emotionally highly charged public arguments about politics, vaccination, standards of beauty and body image, climate change, vegetarianism, etc. Such arguments are seldom on point, and if you look closely, most heated arguments quickly slide into opponents blaming and shaming each other for their personal qualities: "You are blind, delusional, an idiot, a personification of pure evil."

Yet it is often down to a perspective that you take. As much as the following Internet memes might be a cliché, they are remarkably accurate—our disagreements often have more to do with our vantage point than with our personal qualities.

Memes about differences of opinions

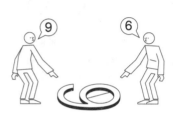 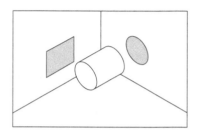

In my line of work, I have interviewed more than 200 remarkably accomplished people from different walks of life and all across the globe. I have had to interview some people with whom I strongly disagree. When you have a camera and sound rolling and hundreds of people watching, and your guest drops a phrase that makes your skin crawl, the idea that helps me is very simple: my goal is to understand my guest, look deep into their mind and heart, and see the essence of that person. I made a surprising discovery—despite such a strikingly diverse style of presenting our ideas, deep down inside most people are very similar—they want to be good and do good. We are just a bit different in how we see the trajectory to that noble destination, to be good and do good. But in essence, I have seen lost souls and miserable souls, but almost never an "evil incarnate," as we sometimes think about our opponents.

Rule number two is a hard one—acceptance. Can you accept another person the way they are? Can you let go of all your expectations toward another person? Can you let go of your expectations of how another person needs to be, act, behave, think, and talk?

You have the right to be you, and they have the right to be them. When you go into a dialogue, don't expect anything from other people—not to think or feel in a certain way, not to express themselves the way you would like, not even to believe you or agree with you.

Now, expand this principle to the closest people in your life—can you coexist with your loved ones without having any expectations toward them, without telling them what they must do, how they must think, which decisions they must take?

The moment you let go of all expectations toward other people, your relationship with them transforms beyond imaginable. When Vishen and I separated, my biggest surprise was how much our relationship had improved once I stopped thinking along the lines of "You have to do this because you are my husband." We let go of all the claims on each other, and the air cleared, and we finally had the willingness and the freedom to communicate as two equal and independent souls. This shift requires trust and letting go of your desire to control other people.

This rule, of course, does not imply that you cannot have expectations regarding your own boundaries.

3. NONVIOLENCE

The next rule is easily observable if you master the previous one. It is incredibly powerful, not very obvious for people with strong natural inclination toward honesty, and one of my favourites. I wish more people adhered to it, but even this wish is a violation of one of the rules.

The nonviolence rule is really very simple: no judging, teaching, preaching, or fixing. It is based on the same fundamental idea as the prior rule—you have the right to be you, and your opponent has the right to be them.

This rule is challenged during heated discussions and arguments. When you hear someone sharing their experience and expressing their point of view, it is often irresistibly tempting to "show them the right way." It is so obvious when someone else makes a mistake, and with all your good intentions, you really want to help. But if your advice and help is unasked for, unsolicited, or even unwelcome, it will not serve the purpose. Furthermore, it is a form of violence.

When you feel drawn to share your valuable advice, it is good to remember that what you are sharing is just your version of the truth, and it may be not absolute, or not timely, or not acceptable to your opponent. That, of course, does not mean that you cannot share your point of view—that is what arguments are about, after all. But a point of view is a very different expression from judgement, teaching, preaching, or fixing.

A point of view is an independent opinion expressed into the open space. It will influence those who are ready to hear and change, and it will be unheeded by those who are not. It is a nonviolent expression of an idea with no judgement passed and no attempts made to manipulate others.

Yet, to practise this rule in your daily life, outside the context of public discussions with relative strangers, you need a great deal of faith and trust toward other people, and an ability to let go of your desire to control and manage others. And sometimes, it will mean witnessing your loved ones in pain. Are you ready?

Here's a real-life example from my own experience:

It happened one Sunday night, when we came back home after a short family trip to the islands in Malaysia. I walked into my son's room and found him crying in bed. We had been traveling, and because of this, he hadn't done his homework. It may seem like a relatively inconsequential issue for an adult, but the humiliation and fear for an 11-year-old may well be quite mortifying in situations such as this.

It was painful to watch my boy so inconsolably sad and scared. And my natural instinct was to rush in and save the day, to write to the teacher immediately, explain the situation, take the blame for traveling all weekend rather than staying put doing class assignments. In other words, to manipulate the situation somewhat violently. But would that have been the best thing for Hayden?

No, I concluded. So, rather than fixing the situation for my son, I offered all I had to help him deal with it on his own.

It is a simple enough incident, with no hard consequences, just a few tears and my uneasy heart. Yet, we do exactly the same in more complex scenarios with much more serious outcomes—when our loved ones have bad habits; go through grief or difficult times; experience painful emotions, problems, and complications in life; when they make stupid decisions or idiotic mistakes. Our natural tendency is to do our best to solve all those problems for our loved ones—to teach them, preach and fix them, and judge them along the way.

In my case, it took years of hard-earned wisdom inspired by my teachers to finally realise that every one of us has their own journey. Everyone has one, my children included, even if sometimes I have to see them in pain, they need their journeys. Witnessing my loved ones in pain became my journey, and most likely, I too need this journey.

So what do you do? Do you stand aside and witness your loved one in pain?

The short answer is yes, you stand aside and witness.

But the more complex answer is—you stand by, you have their back, you keep having faith and trust in those whom you love, you keep your light on for them. But you don't fix it for them.

When Hayden came from school the next day, he was completely fine—the mortifying situation was resolved, and he did it without my interference. He walked his journey, got his lessons, and moved on. I didn't rob Hayden of his experience and his journey, as much as I wanted to fix it for him. Because guess what? If your loved one is having an experience, it is because they need to learn some lessons. And if you fix their journey for them, those lessons are going to catch up and hit your loved one later . . . when you might not be near to keep your light on for them.

And with this, rule number three in the Open Dialogue, and in life at large, is: Don't fix, teach, preach, and judge. Practise nonviolence.

4. NO STORIES

Open Dialogue is a practise of being in the present moment. One of the rules declares that you only express your present emotions, what you are feeling right now, with as much honesty and sincerity as you can manage. No stories. No deeper explanations.

This is another simple rule with deep philosophical roots. Here's why:

Have you ever felt somewhat ashamed of your emotions? You say, "No, thank you! I don't feel like having tea," and you feel compelled to go on with your explanation that you had a late lunch and you are still full to the brim, or that tea makes you feel alert and it is too late in the day.

Often when we express ourselves sincerely, we feel the need to qualify our emotions, as if feeling what you feel just because you feel it is not enough. As if you need to apologise and excuse a candid expression of your feelings. As if shame and guilt need to be felt when you are being open, honest, and sincere.

This rule, if you look into the essence of it, gives you permission to feel whatever you feel without any qualifying explanations and apologies for being honest and sincere. It is a liberation, letting you off the hook of your own stories, forgiveness for the audacity to be yourself.

In the context of Open Dialogue, this rule means that you do not go into telling stories from the past, even if the past is just this morning or half an hour ago. You only express how you feel in the present moment, and you stay in that present moment with your present emotions unapologetically.

A beautiful nuance of this rule is that you will notice the fluidity of your emotions if you let go of your past stories and only focus on what you are feeling at the present moment. Often it is our attachment to the past and our stories that keep us stuck with a particular emotion.

But in real life, this rule is a little harder to follow. We keep wanting to apologise, explain, and qualify our own feelings. And here's an important distinction: it is okay to explain and qualify your actions, your words, your decisions. But your emotions are not *you*, they are not your choice or your decision; they are signals that you are to hear and interpret. So apologising for something, which, strictly speaking, is not under your control,[22] is nonsensical.

So how do you practise this rule in everyday life? Try this as an experiment:

- Do not apologise for how you feel. Keep apologies for your actions and decisions, not your emotions.

- Do not shame or blame yourself for your emotions. Remember that your task is to control your reaction to emotions, not the emotions per se.

- Let go of your past stories. Do not explain how you feel now linked to what you have experienced before.

To be fair, the last point may require professional help to accomplish. Some past traumas do keep haunting people for years, and they may need professional therapy or even medication to get over such traumatic experiences and learn to move on with life. But for most of us, people living rather ordinary lives, the temptation to hold on to our past stories is limiting our future transformation.

I was born in the wrong country, my family was poor, my boyfriend dumped me, my wife broke my heart—not only do we explain current emotions with past stories, but often, our past stories write our future ones.

5. SINCERITY

Many superhero movies start with the origin story, in which the future hero is only just discovering his or her superpowers. Do you remember how young Clark Kent flew into walls or Peter Parker messed up his spiderwebs?[23] Superpowers need to be understood, mastered, and sometimes harnessed, because even great powers can become disastrous. On a more practical note, think of the many amazing resources which were developed for the benefit of humanity, but turned into a disaster as a result of being wrongly used. From guns, which were turned on innocent people; to nuclear power, which sometimes wipes out entire cities;[24] to planes, which occasionally crash; to drugs, which are overprescribed for the benefit of the pharmaceutical industry.[25] We could go on and on.

Even intrinsically good things can become deadly weapons if they are wrongly handled, overused, or misapplied. And honesty is definitely a powerful weapon, which can crush and destroy if it is used unkindly.

I believe that almost any good quality in a human being, if it is taken to the extreme, can turn evil, or, in a less dramatic way, become destructive. Too much kindness might become submissive, too much love might become possessive, too much joy might become delirious and manic, etc., etc. Yet we live in a society that doesn't think that there is such a thing as too much honesty.

If honesty is foremost about relationships, then it is apt to quote one of our time's most prominent relationship experts, Esther Perel, a psychotherapist who has devoted herself to understanding infidelity. In an interview with blogger Jay Shetty, Esther shares the worst relationship advice ever given to couples—to always tell the truth to your partner.[26]

On that note, it is important to remark that I do not use *honesty* and *truth* interchangeably. While telling (your version of) the truth is usually a consequence of honesty, honesty is not always about telling the truth. You can be honest without knowing the truth. You can be honest without sharing the truth. And (plot twist) I wonder if you could tell the truth without being honest?

Since honesty is a skill to be mastered and truth is often dependent on the truth-teller's particular point of view, I chose the word *sincerity* for this rule. It has a nuance that neither honesty nor truth can cover. Sincerity is an intention to be honest: it is an expression of self in accordance with one's own feelings and beliefs. Sincerity doesn't claim to know the truth, and so it doesn't have the inconsiderate bluntness of truth-telling. And sincerity is an internal phenomenon—it is a type of honesty about the self, so it doesn't have the interpersonal aspect implied in the traditional usage of the word *honesty*.

This rule is very simple: be as sincere as you can. Speak and behave in accordance with your inner world, your beliefs, thoughts, desires, and values. In other words, be true to yourself.

6. PERSONAL PRACTISE

Maybe counterintuitively, Open Dialogue is a personal practise, even if it is practised in a group. You practise honesty for yourself, not for the group. You clear your system, and your result does not depend on whether or not the group is on the same wavelength with you. Your group is just your mirror.

It is when you start seeing the world as your own reflection when you truly master self-honesty. And this idea is not a pleasant pill to swallow, but let's take it step by step.

Let me introduce you to yet another fashionable buzzword: *empathy*. It is an ability to feel and understand another person's emotions and experiences. But there is one little nuance: you can only feel or understand what is familiar to you. You can understand love if you have felt love. You can understand grief if you have felt grief. You can understand self-hatred if you have hated yourself. But if you have never experienced an emotion, you can only imagine how it feels.

You may imagine how it feels to have an eating disorder, but you cannot recall the feeling if you have not experienced it. You might imagine how it feels to live with a disability, but you cannot know it if you are able-bodied. I may imagine how it feels to be a person of colour living in a white-privilege world, but I cannot say that I know how it really feels. This mirror effect is exactly why people are often unconscious about their biases. They can imagine, they can rely on their empathic ability, but they don't know the feeling because they have not experienced it.

If you have experienced personal-growth training, you might have done this connection exercise called "I see it in your eyes." You walk around a room with other people, stop in front of one of them, look them in the eye and "see their feelings"—maybe insecurities, or fears, pain, joy, love, whichever is the choice of your facilitator. This is a feel-good exercise, and it makes you feel seen, heard, understood, and connected. But the interesting minor detail is that you cannot really see more in the eyes of your partner than what you have personally experienced.

We certainly do have an empathic ability and even intuition with the people closest to us. I could always recognise my husband's emotions when he was on stage, even if I was across the room from him. But I could only "feel" his emotions through my own prism of experiences. So, if I recognised passion, it was because I had experienced it in a similar setting. If I recognised insecurity, it was my own past experience that I could see in him.

And since it is only the reflections of our own experiences that we recognise in the people around us, it is logical to assume that we may be wrong at times. We may misinterpret another person, take their contemplative mood for shyness, or their nervousness for arrogance, and so on.

In the context of the Open Dialogue, this rule means that whatever you experience during the discussion is all yours. You may imagine it is coming from another person, but it is your own reflection, and another person is just a trigger of your own experiences, often triggering you unconsciously.

In real life, this rule means that you must take full responsibility for your experiences. It is not the world forcing you to be a certain way or making you do certain things; it is not other people making you feel certain emotions. Your perception of other people and the world around you is a reflection of your own experiences and whatever you feel, do, or are.

In a more practical way, you only have a problem with other people to the extent that you have a problem with yourself.

Reflection Points

For this chapter, I am giving you an exercise on clarity. To do justice to my friend's Open Dialogue method, you would have to learn and practise the principles at a live event with a certified instructor. However, even following just the first principle—clarity of the goal—will make a big difference in your life.

Next time you find yourself in an argument, pause for a moment and ask yourself: What is my goal in this argument?

- Do you want to prove that you are right? And consequently, that your opponent is wrong?

- Do you want to change your opponent's point of view, words, actions, feelings?

- Do you want to understand your opponent?

- Do you want to find a solution to a partic-ular situation?

Only go on with your argument, or discussion, once you are clear about your own goal in this communication.

PART VI

Kindness

A
HEALING
Tandem

Be kind whenever possible. It is always possible.

— DALAI LAMA XIV[1]

There is one personal growth practise that I find easy in theory, but near-on impossible in my unembellished life—practising love for *all* people.

It is a beautiful idealistic endeavour, and, taken out of context, it is uplifting and heartwarming. The idea is that you have to extend your love beyond your closest circle of people that you love effortlessly, beyond your friends and family, to every single person alive—people you know, people you don't know, and even your enemies and people who have wronged you. But the moment your mind hovers over a real-life example of someone who is hard to love, the whole idea starts sounding silly.

Let's do a small mental exercise. But you have to be completely honest with your feelings, not pretending and not stretching the truth.

- Imagine the person that you love the most. Focus on the love that you feel for them. How does it feel?

- Now, imagine a person who has hurt you, wronged you, maybe even dislikes you. Imagine expanding your love to that person. How does it feel?

- Compare the two feelings. Can you truthfully
  say that your feelings did not change? That love
  for someone who has hurt you feels similar to
  love in the first example?

If these two expressions of love didn't feel quite the
same, don't worry, you are not a horrible human being
incapable of true and unconditional love. Not at all! You
are a normal human being with real and unfeigned emotions. I believe that the closest we can come to experiencing pure, unconditional love is when we learn to love our
own children. But sincere love for all people is a hard skill
to develop. It is not for everyone, and I am not sure if it
should be.

Love is a wonderful skill, and I wish we all knew how to
practise it properly. But where love fails, kindness remains.

Sincere kindness can be expressed in any circumstances when love cannot. You don't need to love someone to be kind to them. You don't need to condone or
respect someone to be kind to them. You don't even need
to truly care, but you can still be kind. You can be kind
when you are sad, grieved, upset, and angry. You can
always be kind. Always.

When you express kindness, your soul, your mind will
not suspect falsehood and deceit—the act of kindness is
enough to be absolutely sure that what you express is pure.

Yet, kindness is a vastly disregarded and undervalued
quality that we seldom hear about. Hence, this section is
dedicated to this missing piece of the puzzle—the complementary concept to honesty: kindness.

It is easy to be honest about pleasing things. Even if we
are not used to expressing our warmest feelings to other
people and may feel awkward telling someone that we like
and appreciate them, the essence of the message feels good

nevertheless. It is gratifying to bear the good news and be liked and appreciated for it.

Yet there is a reason why we beg "Don't shoot the messenger!" because no one likes a messenger who brings bad news. Being honest about things that are not pleasant calls for caution and a special approach. And you might have heard about such techniques as the "feedback sandwich" or principles of nonviolent communication, which teach algorithms and proper phraseology, even choice of words, for practising dangerous kinds of honesty.

You are, essentially, advised to build up your communication in such a way that the piece of honesty is "cushioned" to be less shocking.

Yet, like the princess and the pea,[2] your ego will get bruised even if the pea of bad news is hidden under layers and layers of down and feathers.

If you were to present a piece of bad news without any embellishments, could you do it with such kindness and compassion that it would heal the wound as soon as your honesty caused it?

Since I am an entrepreneur with years of experience, part and parcel of the role is giving bad news to people I care about. And the worst is firing them. Once, I had to let go of half of our people all at once. It wasn't a pleasant task, but it needed doing, and what's more, it was my job to do it.

I once heard a good friend share her story of being fired. Her job was in finance, and she was really bad at it—diligent, eager, but really bad—because her real passions were elsewhere. One day, her manager called her in to share the bad news: she was being let go. My friend asked, "Are you firing me?" and her manager replied, "No, dear, I am not. I am setting you free to pursue your passion."

You see, it's not the words, nor the cushioning, nor the setting. It's not about the sh*t sandwich. The point is in your intention. Do you wish the one who is to receive your bad news well?

My friend's manager cared about her and wished her the best. That, of course, wasn't why she was fired, but it made a big difference in the messaging. And that example was what helped me in delivering my share of bad news. If kindness is in the heart of the message, the wound will start healing as soon as the blow is dealt. It is hard to let go of people who have worked with you, but if they don't thrive, if they don't live to their potential, if they are whiling away their time and hidden talent where neither are truly valued, then the separation may be done kindly, because it is ultimately better to "let another free to pursue their passion," even if it hurts them at first.

Honesty, no matter how necessary, has to be laden with kindness. For honesty without kindness is mean, cruel, and unhelpful.

And honesty which is masquerading to look like care and compassion is the worst kind, because it is actually gaslighting, a farce, and not really honest. It's like "tough love," which is neither love nor honesty.

I am often criticised by my (usually Russian) audience for how I look and how I dress. But without kindness, such comments give me nothing. I cannot make myself more beautiful or dress to please everyone, so there is no hope for improvement in such criticism. And delivered without kindness or compassion, such "truths" are hurtful and unhelpful.[3]

Yet kindness without honesty is also flawed, as it quickly becomes flattery. And flattery is a gateway to manipulation. There is a big difference between a sincere compliment coming from the heart and pleasantries and niceties, which are liberally shared just to make you feel good. While you might appreciate the effort of someone pleasing you, there is something unsettling about insincerity. If you have ever been lavishly praised for something trivial, you know how uncomfortable it feels.

And so, honesty and kindness have to go in tandem, since neither is any good without the other.

Reflection Points

This exercise is called "A Compliment Challenge."

Give out five compliments, preferably to random people, not your closest friends. Compliment them sincerely; feel the admiration; don't just say pleasantries. It's all about the honesty and kindness tandem, not one without the other.

You don't have to tell your compliments to these people if you are not comfortable. Sincerity is more important in this exercise than the courage of saying a compliment.

Self-Kindness

You cannot see the stars from the bottom of a ditch.

— KATERINA KALCHENKO[1]

Why is self-honesty such a hard feat? There are two reasons why being honest with yourself may be daunting.

First, you may be afraid of what you will discover if you are fully honest with yourself. Which dragons will you uncover in your basement? Will you be able to make friends with those hidden dragons and continue coexisting with them?

Second, you may be afraid of the changes in your life that self-honesty will inevitably bring about. You will be a changed person, so, naturally, you will want to change your life. Are you ready for these changes? Do you even want to rock a perfectly sound boat in the first place?

You will need kindness to deal with that first fear and courage to work with the second.

Coincidentally or not, these are my two favourite qualities in people: courage and kindness. It is a beautiful mix, almost like yin and yang, almost contradictory, although the words are not antonymous, and the qualities are actually complementary. For the word *courage* comes from old French *corage* and Latin *cor*, which means "heart," and the heart is the central organ both in courage and in kindness.

So, we'll dig deeper into kindness, especially self-kindness, and then move on to courage later. And, traditionally, we'll focus on your relationship with yourself and then expand it to the rest of the world.

When I decided that I was done feeling guilty and ashamed for being me, when I plucked up courage to grab a flashlight and go searching behind the beautiful, flawless facade of my perfectly Instagrammable life, that was when I wandered into the most obscure and neglected corners of my psyche and shined that flashlight into the darkest corners. It was determination to be kind to myself, no matter what I discovered, that helped me along in this journey.

Some people believe that you have to be critical toward yourself, hold yourself to a higher standard, expect more from yourself, and only then will you be able to grow, evolve, and transform for the better. The idea is that you will not become better if you are too kind toward yourself, almost complacent. "Don't you need to be dissatisfied, even angry with yourself to want to change?" I've been asked. The guy insisted that self-criticism, even at times self-hate, was necessary for progress.

I find this idea dangerously misleading, and I believe that we can thank marketers for this deep-rooted misconception. Marketing is often built around pain points: "What is the thought that keeps you up all night?" Marketers look for pain, make you relate to it, intensify the feeling, and then offer you a simple, magic-pill solution. You will see such an approach in other areas in life too. Take the old adage in the media that "good news doesn't sell," or the entertainment industry, which is often built around scandal. We've been trained to see pain and conflict as a necessary condition to trigger change and transformation. But I find this approach erroneous. Let me explain.

Hitting rock bottom might inspire you to look for a different way to live your life. Intense pain might become your motivation to avoid such pain in the future, and that will make you change too. These are great movie scripts but, unfortunately, not proven scenarios in real life. What doesn't kill you might make you stronger or tougher, but not necessarily better. It may make you more resilient to adversity and more thick-skinned, more cynical, and less prone to expectations, more pessimistic, more indifferent, and it may even leave you with lifelong trauma. Furthermore, and somewhat gruesomely, what doesn't kill you immediately may still kill you a little later.

I had a wonderful classmate in school. He was a popular kid—smart, ambitious, good-looking—he had all the makings of a huge success. But his life broke him early: his wife left him, and as if one heartbreak wasn't enough, his parents died one after the other. My former classmate went into a deep depression, took to drinking, and lost interest in his business. It was a sad story of spiralling down until the man died at the young age of 42 from overconsumption of alcohol . . . and he was discovered one week later in a dreadful state, with only a faithful dog by his side. It is a gruesome story, maybe a little graphic, but not terribly exceptional in ordinary life. Disappointment, loss, and trauma often lead to more disappointment and, unfortunately, to a downward spiral.

There is no guarantee of growth and betterment in painful experiences, in reaching rock bottom, in dissatisfaction and even anger.

Once, when Hayden was still a little boy, I remember being shocked at his perceptiveness when he casually commented on a twist in a movie plot: "This guy has been hurt so much, he must be the main villain." And Hayden was right. The guy did become the main villain, just as so many other famous villains, such as Darth Vader, Lex

Luthor, or Uriah Heep (a classic example), who turned bad from enduring too much pain. Hurt people hurt people. It is excessive pain that makes most people do bad things to other people.[5]

Thus, thinking that perfectionism, self-criticism, placing a high bar for yourself, shame and guilt, or even anger and hate turned toward yourself will make you want to become better is a slippery slope. When one of our wonderful Mindvalley teachers, Marisa Peer, was recording her program with us, a videographer asked her during a break between shooting: "Marisa, if I keep telling myself that I am enough, won't I become stagnant? Won't I lie back on my sofa and do nothing but tell myself that I am enough the way I am?"

Here's what Marisa replied to that (in my loose interpretation): "You lie back on your sofa doing nothing, not because you think that you are good enough, but the opposite—you do that because you are afraid that you are *not* enough. It is a fear of failure, of not being good enough, that prevents you from going out and exposing yourself to the world, doing something courageous and meaningful. When you know that you are enough, you find courage to go out and challenge yourself."

Change is not a natural consequence of pain; it is often a sign of healing. Only when you are ready to heal will you find in you what it takes to start growing again. And that moment is marked with kindness.

Transformation starts with kindness toward yourself. Kindness gives you courage to be honest with yourself and wisdom to accept yourself the way you are. It will also give you the certainty that you have what it takes to go out and be brave and become better.

We have now come to the most important part of this book: how to learn to be kind toward yourself. Let's talk about self-love.

Reflection Points

This will be a very enjoyable exercise, I promise. We'll start with the first part of the exercise, and after the next chapter, we'll do the second part.

In your diary, list all the ways you express and show love for yourself.

Ready?

Now let's talk about self-love.

SELF-CARE
VS.
Self-Love

To love oneself is the beginning of a lifelong romance.

— OSCAR WILDE[6]

When a baby is born, she cannot survive on her own. A baby needs someone to take care of her: someone to feed her, wash her, dress her, put her to sleep, walk with her. But more than that, a baby needs love: someone to hear and understand her, someone to soothe her when she cries, someone to laugh and play with her, someone to hold her, someone to show her the world.

Love and care are rather different. Both are needed and important. But care is easy to see and measure, while love is somewhat intangible. A baby needs to be taken care of. Nannies, caretakers, doctors, nurses, teachers, and parents, of course, do the caretaking. But you will not raise a happy, confident, and mentally healthy child without love, no matter how much care you put on that child.

I like to compare self-love with love for a baby, because it is so easy to get distracted by care and pampering and miss the essence. Love is not about washing, feeding, and walking with a baby—it is about loving the baby through a physically challenging pregnancy and delivery, through sleepless nights, through exhaustion, confusion, and frustration. It is a relationship, not just an act of service.

So, with that pretext, let me ask you a question: How do you love yourself?

It is a tricky question, even if you have this context. Often, when we talk about self-love, we actually mean self-care. A lot of self-love rituals and practises mix up love for oneself with taking care of one's mind and body. Both are important, mind you, but I want to focus on the deeper and a little more complex of the pair: self-love.

Before we dive into it, let me linger a bit on the distinction between the two and why it is important to see the difference.

Self-care is usually skin-deep (massage, facial, manicure), while self-love penetrates much deeper. Self-care relies on rituals (exercise, meditation, walk), while self-love is a constant attitude, and so there is no big harm in missing self-care from time to time—you can pick it up where you dropped it off.

Missing self-love, on the other hand, can cause real immediate damage. Self-care is about taking time for yourself, indulging yourself, pampering yourself, while self-love doesn't take any time, but it permeates your life every single moment. Self-care is often physical, whereas self-love doesn't really have a physical component. But most importantly, if you get caught up in self-care, you might miss the depth and essence of self-love.

Coming back to my initial analogy—you can shower your child with gifts, expensive toys, nice treats, and lavish birthday parties, but what your child really needs is your presence. Fifteen minutes of your undivided time focused on her are much more valuable than an army of good nannies, teachers, and a pedigree puppy for a pet. Conscious parents know about this trap: You cannot compensate for your missing love for the child with gifts. It simply doesn't work like that. And just because your child has everything she needs in the material world, does not quench her need for love and connection.

And so it is with self-care and self-love. No amount of self-care can compensate for the lack of self-love. You can be in excellent physical shape because you exercise vigorously, eat healthy, sleep well, take time for meditation, take walks in nature, and get massages; you can pamper yourself with spa treatments and occasional shopping and do all the proper rituals of self-care; but none of it adds much to how you actually feel about yourself deep inside.

Acknowledging that you deserve to take time for yourself is not the same as loving yourself even if you failed to prioritise taking time for yourself. You will charge your phone not out of love for this particular piece of machinery, but because you wouldn't be able to use it if its battery was flat.

Self-care is about surviving, while self-love is about thriving.

Self-care is incredibly important—you should take care of your body; it is the temple of your soul. But if you were to err and fall, can you still love yourself? If you were to fail your strict diet, or stay up all night indulging in a movie, or skip your yoga class, or wake up one day feeling cranky and moody, would you be able to still love yourself?

I would like to argue that the harm that your failing of a self-care ritual would cause to your body is not as grave as your blaming, shaming, and disappointed self-talk. That excessive glass of wine is not as bad for your body as hating yourself for it. That lack of sleep and sluggishness is not as bad for your future as you panicking and beating yourself up for it.

Your self-care will never compensate for your self-love, but your self-love will always trump self-care any day.

Oh dear! I'm in dangerous territory again. I can hear the questions: "But if I love myself despite all my flaws and mistakes, isn't this a slippery slope too? Won't I indulge and fail and keep loving myself even if I am out of shape, lazy, and doing absolutely nothing about my life?"

Let's come back to my favourite analogy. Do you feel the difference between a loving parent and an indulging parent? Do you feel the difference between a loving parent and a parent who would let their child do anything as long as she doesn't bother them?

- "Oh well! Keep watching cartoons, as long as you eat!"
- "Have that toy if you must, just stop making a fuss!"
- "Here, play this game—just let mom have a chat with a friend!"

Every modern parent knows that an iPad is an emergency measure in times of crisis when you don't have capacity for good parenting. And so it is in your relationship with yourself. Self-indulgence is a substitute for the times when you don't have the capacity for proper self-love.

Reflection Points

This is the second part of the exercise we did right before this chapter. Bring out your list of ways you show love for yourself. Next to each item on your list, write if it is:

- Self-care
- Self-love
- Indulging

The last one, obviously, is something that makes you feel good, but isn't good for you in the long run or in excess.

Since self-love is by definition not ritualistic, you are likely not going to have a lot of self-love present in your list. But you can think of the ways to nurture more true, deep self-love in your life.

YOU CANNOT
Overdose
ON SELF-LOVE

*We can't be so desperate for love that we
forget where we can always find it; within.*

— ALEXANDRA ELLE[7]

Can you guess what the one question I get asked the most
is? It might have crossed your mind already.

When does self-love become selfish?

We are used to believing that selfishness is an extreme
expression of self-love. But it is a misunderstanding. Selfishness is the exact opposite of self-love. Let's look deeper
into the two phenomena.

Do you remember our mechanical physics class in the
beginning of this book? Let's go back to that class and
make some simple analogies to illustrate the concept that
I'm trying to explain.

If you were a vessel, a glass, for example, and love was
water, then self-love would be the water within the glass.
Now, if your glass was filled to the brim, you would not be
able to pour more water in it, would you?

But let's say that there was space in the glass. A lot of
it. In that case, you'd have to take your water from somewhere, let's say someone else's cup, to fill yours. So the
water you'd add that isn't from your own source would
be selfishness.

As you can see, although selfishness can look very
similar to self-love at times, only this kind does not

originate from within. Selfishness means that you need to get love, attention, care, and special treatment from people around you.

And so, I declare that selfishness is the exact opposite of self-love, because it is virtually impossible if you have enough love for yourself when your vessel is filled to the brim. Selfishness only happens when there is space in you, when you don't love yourself well enough and you need someone else to fill that void.

So can you overdose on self-love? I think the answer is clear—you cannot. There is no such thing as too much self-love. In fact, I think that all the distorted expressions that we often confuse with self-love are not only poor substitutes; they are indicators that your love for yourself is wavering.

Obsession over self-care, indulgence, and selfishness are simply attempts to compensate for something that is lacking—self-love.

So what is self-love, then, if it is not selfishness and indulgence? I am not an expert on love, but let me give it a try and define what I mean by self-love.

My kids are my biggest teachers. When Hayden was born, I was reborn with him, as a human, as a woman, as a soul on this planet. I am a little idealistic when it comes to parent-child relationships, and I am aware that there are too many exceptions to the rule, but I do believe that the closest you may come to experiencing pure, unconditional, selfless love is when you learn to love your child.

And so, in love, my golden standard is love for my children. If in doubt, I imagine and ask myself, how would I feel, or think, or react, if that particular situation was happening with one of my own children? And could I love myself as unconditionally as I could them?

Here's an example:

Sometime after my 40th birthday, I started noticing the inevitable changes in my body—the few extra kilograms that refused to go away, the wrinkles near my eyes and the folds around my mouth, the grey hair flashing in the mirror. Over the following years, I caught myself thinking thoughts like: "I just need to lose this soft belly, and fill in my lashes, and maybe, I should consider what's good on the market for younger-looking skin . . ."

Wanting to look good is a natural desire for both men and women. And without diverging into a very important discussion about contemporary beauty standards and women's body image, let me just say this—there is nothing wrong with wanting to look good. Exaggeration and obsession are dangerous, but everyone takes a shower and combs their hair on a daily basis—it has more to do with our looks than actual health benefits.

I think I still love my body with its extra weight and signs of ageing, but in the back of my mind, I have those nagging thoughts along the lines of "if only I could change a few nuances, then I would be 100 percent on board with my body."

Just for context—by no standards am I overweight, but I am not wearing size XS as I used to in my 20s. In fact, my body has made huge progress since then: I have learned to swim at 35 and to ride a bike at 43, I have improved my strength, and I am really progressing in boxing, and, best of all, I have birthed and nursed two children—none of these could I say about myself at age 25. My only advantage was youth and a size or two smaller clothes.

It was only when I thought of my gold standard in love that I truly understood the meaning of loving one's body. If I were to replace "my body" with "my child," would I still have that nagging thought of "if only I could change a few nuances?"

The answer was clear to me. I would never imagine thinking that I love Hayden, but I would love him more if he didn't have Asperger's. Or that I would love Eve more if she had grey eyes like my mom. I love my children the way they are. I would not change *anything* about them. Nothing in the world would make me love them more than I already do.

Yet, when it comes to my body, I have 101 conditions to fulfil before I can grant it my full love. I don't think such love is unconditional, or even pure. It sounds more like a bargain: "If you lose those cursed few kilograms, I will give you my love."

I believe that pure love is not a bargain. It has no conditions. It is accepting, and it doesn't seek benefit. Can I love myself, beyond just my body? Can I love my personality, my humanness, my mind, and my soul the way I have learned to love my children? No bargain?

And it is the same lack of self-love that creates distorted relationships. We then seek to fill that void by seeking validation, admiration, love, and acceptance from others:

"Do you think I am too fat in this outfit?"

"Do you think this is a good piece of writing?"

"Am I a good friend/husband/father?"

Ultimately: "Am I worthy of love?"

We often seek the answers to these questions from outside, and this becomes the condition for us to grant ourselves full love. So, on one side, we do buy into the idea of self-love, but on the other, we give it a condition: if I can conquer the world, then I'll be worthy of loving myself fully. Before I truly deserve it, too much self-love is selfish, arrogant, delusional, and everything that is wrong. And the appraisal of the worthiness has to come from the outside or else it is not objective. And so, this kind of bargaining self-love turns into a vicious circle.

Pure love doesn't come with conditions, and it doesn't have to be earned. Pure love is given (to a child, at least) just by virtue of someone being in your life. You are, and therefore I love you. It is as simple as this:

Can you love yourself just because you *are*?

Can you love yourself without conditions?

Can you give yourself your love before you have "earned" it?

Can you stop worrying about not growing just because you love yourself with your dragons, flaws, and imperfections?

Can you love yourself not *despite* your dragons, flaws, and imperfections, but *with* them?

Unfortunately, we are trained for conditional love early on. We are praised when we behave well. We are punished when we do wrong. And often, in such transactions, love is the currency—love is given as reward and withdrawn as punishment.

Naturally, when we grow up, we carry on this pattern: we use love as currency and dole it out in accordance to how our expectations in relationships are being met. And, of course, we carry that same pattern into our relationship with ourselves. And it is this conditional attitude to giving love that creates all sorts of distortions, from selfishness and indulgence to self-hate.

Loving yourself is a skill you have to master if you want to live a happy life—in fact, if you want to live a happy, meaningful, and fulfilled life, because self-love is the beginning of true transformation.

But if loving yourself is a little hard at this particular moment in life, or if it is hard in certain circumstances or situations, try kindness first. Kindness always works where love fails, as I previously explained, because you can be kind when you are not in the mood, when you are angry or sad, and even when you are not ready for love.

When you cannot love yourself, be kind to yourself. It will do the job for now, and with time, it will teach you true, pure, unconditional self-love, the kind that doesn't need distortions to feel good.

Reflection Points

This exercise is called "Turning Up Self-Love." It is another twist for your moments of awareness. Anchor your awareness to situations when you are slamming a break on your self-love. Maybe you criticise yourself for a failure. Maybe you are angry with yourself for a mistake or a blunder. Maybe you are feeling uncomfortable when you are being publicly praised. Maybe you are dismissing your achievements.

- Pause for a moment and ask yourself: Am I depriving myself of my own love?

- Tell yourself mentally: "I deserve all the love I can give myself!"

PART VII

Courage

A LEAP OF
Faith

Fear is a natural reaction to moving closer to the truth.

— PEMA CHÖDRÖN[1]

I could have started talking about courage a little earlier, because you will need it every step of the way from the very first moment when you embark on the journey back to yourself. You need courage to be honest, to be kind to yourself in the face of your dragons, but most of all, you will need courage when you are ready to present the new you to the world, especially your loved ones.

When I started my journey of self-discovery, it was the inevitable changes that I feared the most. We love the certainty of what we have, even if we would like something more or different. It is often not the fear of conquering new heights that scares us, but the fear of losing what we already have.

We humans do not like uncertainty, and so we fight it. Yet it is exactly because we try to make uncertain things certain that we cause even more problems for ourselves. How does it work out in life?

- You have to have a hard conversation, and you are scared of the consequences. So, rather than making the leap of faith, you play it by ear— you sort of have the hard conversation, but not completely, because you have to leave an escape route for your ego.

- If you are single, like I am at the moment, and you are ready for a relationship, you don't go for the "right one," you play the numbers game— you date a selection of mates hoping that one of them will work out.

- You outgrow your work, you feel that you need new challenges, but rather than leaping into the unknown and starting something new, you keep hovering around the same company, or the same industry, or the same network of people, or the same job, hoping to rediscover yourself in the comfort of familiarity.

It is in human nature to secure the exit routes, to create a little insurance, to have a backup option. And it is probably wise. But wise is not always best.

I like to compare complicated and scary decisions in my life with a skydive. It is so scary, paralysing, almost like a mini-death because you cannot even imagine life on the other side of the unknown. But once you make that first step, you find yourself flying.

You will fly, but you have to make the step into the unknown first—you will have to let go and leap. Imagine that you were trying to skydive, but you wanted to secure an "escape route," a way back? You would end up dangling in the air, more like a bungee jump than a real flying experience.

So why do we keep that bungee cord on when we need to make the leap of faith? Why do we prefer dangling and holding on rather than flying like a bird? Let's talk about making hard decisions and why we avoid them like the plague.

Reflection Points

This exercise is called "Expanding Your Comfort Zone," and you do not need to skydive or bungee jump, unless you want to, of course.

First, make a list of at least 30 things that are outside of your comfort zone. They don't have to be scary or dangerous. "Just outside" your comfort zone is okay. Maybe it is an exotic food you have never tried, or going for a kickboxing class, or just striking a conversation with a stranger. If you get stuck, ask a child to help you with ideas.

Second, do one item on the list every day until you are finished with all items. It will take you at least 30 days or more, since you will start getting ideas as you go through the list.

The point of this exercise is to build your courage muscle—the more you do things that require courage, the easier it is to be brave.

AVOIDING
THE INDECISION
Trap

*Nothing is so exhausting as
indecision, and nothing is so futile.*

— BERTRAND RUSSELL[2]

There is a proverbial crossroad in Russian fairy tales, which I always found puzzling and distressing. There stands a boulder with directions: "Go left—and you lose your horse; go right—and you lose your life; go straight—and you stay alive, but you lose yourself."[3] It is a thoroughly depressing and hopeless choice, and if the deeper meaning of such an inscription might be arguable, the choice itself, unfortunately, is not unfamiliar.

Have you been on this crossroad (figuratively speaking)? Have you been in a situation like this? Whichever road you take, there are losses to be considered. It is a paralysing choice when it happens in real life, and often, rather than making an actual choice of a path to take, we choose indecision.

Indecision sounds like a good idea when you don't know which way to go. Rather than rock the boat and break what's working, we choose to stand there looking at the inscription on the stone and pondering our choices:

- Should I break up with this person?
- Should I have a hard conversation and set my boundaries?
- Should I be honest about my wishes and desires?
- Should I give up this dead-end career and pursue my passion?

Being one step away from a decision is much easier than making the one step into the unknown. So we keep endlessly pondering our choices, looking out for the signs, searching for the answer. The truth is, it's just indecision, or rather, fear of making a decision.

Let me share another piece of anonymous wisdom: failure to make a decision is a decision to be a failure. As cliché as it may be, indecision is, in and of itself, a decision.

You might think that you are postponing a decision, but in reality, you are deciding to do nothing. You are just not yet admitting it to yourself. You might even mask this decision of doing nothing behind a story about "taking this important decision seriously and not rushing into it."

If you remember my story about Ivy, my first business partner, and my long journey to finally summon the courage to break up the relationship that had failed to work three years earlier, this was a story of indecision and fear. I was so afraid of staying alone in business that I was ready to come up with any plausible explanation and keep going on with that indecision.

On the night when I finally found the courage to make the needed and overdue decision, I remember sitting for half an hour over an e-mail that I was composing to Ivy and into which I was pouring out my frustration and dissatisfaction with our partnership. It was a trying time for our company—our main market was in a deep economic crisis, our business was on the verge of bankruptcy, and my partner didn't want to talk to me. I had written a line at the end of my long, emotional e-mail that said something like this: "If that is how things are right now, I think it is better if we part ways."

I was looking at this last line and thinking that I should only send out this e-mail if I truly meant it. Because if I wasn't sure, that line would be just a manipulative attempt to make my partner behave differently.

Finally, I pressed the Send button and went to sleep with a clear conscience and my heart lightened. The next morning, I was standing in my bathroom with a toothbrush, looking at myself in the mirror, and I felt as if I had wings behind my back. I felt happy, excited, ready to fly. I had made the leap of faith.

The decision that I had been dreading for three years had finally been taken and expressed. I didn't worry about my business partner's reaction. It didn't matter if she was going to agree, disagree, argue, or fight; I had made the decision, I was determined, and it finally gave me the confidence to face anything—the economic crisis, the possible bankruptcy, and the probable wrath of my business partner.

The step that I was afraid to make felt so easy and right once I had made it. Coming back to my skydive analogy, this decision felt exactly like my first skydiving experience.

I remember that feeling after booking it. I was in a dreamlike state, detached, excited, and terrified in the knowledge that on that particular day in the future, I was to jump out of a plane at the height of 4,000 metres[4] above the ground. I couldn't think of anything beyond this upcoming experience. And while consciously I knew that tandem skydiving with an experienced instructor is safer than driving to the site itself, I couldn't get over the paralysing fear.

I remember the day when we were to go to the drop zone. I woke up thinking: "I can get up and go there, but it doesn't mean that I have to actually jump. I can decide not to."

We were going through instructions, and I was still thinking that I could decide not to jump.

We were putting on our gear and getting onto the plane, and I was still thinking that I could decide to stay inside the plane and land as usual, strapped in on the plane, not on a parachute.

We were in the clouds, and I was *still* telling myself that I could decide otherwise, that I didn't need to make that one step into the unknown.

You might think that I had made a decision to skydive on the day when I booked my slot, but in reality, I was still plagued with indecision, replacing the one important decision about making the skydive with a myriad of micro-decisions, which were nudging me in the direction of the final leap of faith.

This is how indecision works: it is the voice in your head telling you that you can still turn back, the bridges have not been burned, you can keep doing things the old way, pretending that there has never been that question in your mind: "Should I make the leap of faith?" Until you have made that last step into the abyss and lost the ground under your feet, you feel that you can turn the clocks back, rewind, and start over again.

And then I was standing at the open door of the plane, looking down at the ground 4,000 metres below me, surreal, unrecognisable, distant, as if I was looking at a miniature toy version of the world. And then you get a kick in the back, and you fall out; you are forced to make the step into the abyss and . . . it finally feels like you are flying. In the case of skydiving, you are *actually* flying.

And, even better, you'll get the supportive kick in the back so you have no choice but to fall and make the leap of faith.

The difference between paralysing fear and the feeling of flying is one step into the unknown. All you need is a bit of courage to make the first step.

Reflection Points

Can you think of pending decisions in your life?

Maybe you keep telling yourself, "I don't know what to do," "I wish I knew the answer to this question," "I'm not sure how to make a choice," "I don't know if I need to change anything about the situation."

Notice when you puzzle yourself about making a decision, making a move, and pause for a moment. You don't need to know the right answer, and I'm not asking you to make the final decision. What I want you to do is simply notice such instances of indecision, when you push aside making a choice, acting decisively, or having a conversation, because you think that you don't know the right answer.

Just notice such pending decisions and ask yourself:

- Is my reluctance to make a decision a choice in itself? Is the inaction my actual choice?

Overthinking
YOUR FEAR

You gain strength, courage and confidence by every experience in which you really stop to look fear in the face. You are able to say to yourself, 'I have lived through this horror. I can take the next thing that comes along.' You must do the thing you think you cannot do.

— ELEANOR ROOSEVELT[5]

I was doing a ropes course at a personal growth event this one time.

Have you ever experienced it yourself? It is a great way to practise courage. And it is a safe kind of practise—you have a harness and professionals making sure that you are doing the right thing. But you are high up above the ground: 5–10 metres,[6] sometimes even higher.

It requires courage—you climb a tree, walk on a tightrope, look down, and realise how crazy the situation really is.

And then, suddenly, the instructor asks: "Who wants to do this course blindfolded?"

I was the first one to volunteer. And so I was to do all the same things, but blindfolded—climb up a tree, 5-10 metres above the ground, walk on a tightrope, get down.

How do you think it felt? It is scary to do a ropes course with full control of your vision and other functions. How do you think it feels to do a thoroughly scary thing blindfolded?

If you think it was even worse, you are mistaken.

I felt at peace.

I felt that way because I was blissfully unaware. I couldn't see the height; I couldn't see how much farther I had to move; I couldn't see that I was up in the air hanging on a bunch of ropes. All I had to do was take the next step. All I felt was my body, my hands and my legs, the tree, the rope, and just the physical contact with a few things that were keeping me up in the air. I could feel the support, but I didn't see the insanity of my situation.

I am an overthinker. My brain loves feeding me the most pessimistic and dreadful scenarios. But when I was up in the air blindfolded, I realised that sometimes you have to focus on the next step, and only on the next step. And sometimes, it helps when you stop obsessing about the big picture.

Courage is an easily trainable skill. And the way to train it is to practise. To become more courageous, literally, you have to start doing things that you are naturally afraid of. And there is no reason to be reckless or risk your life. No point at all! Even though my earlier examples fit into the category of extreme sports, life itself is not an extreme sport.

We are seldom afraid of really dangerous things, such as cancer, heart attacks, or our daily commute. We are usually afraid of things that cannot kill us—public speaking, spiders, or being rejected on a date.

"Fear has big eyes,"[7] or so a Russian saying goes. Your brain's task is to keep you safe from harm, and one way to do so is to scare you off potentially risky undertakings. Have you ever noticed how doting moms overdo the game of keeping their children safe? "Don't climb there; you'll fall down." "Don't pick it up from the floor! Drop it! You'll get germs on your hands!" "Don't run around like crazy or you will smash into a wall!" "Don't do this. Don't do that." You are trained in seeing danger everywhere from a very early age, and your brain keeps playing the doting overprotective mom for the rest of your life.

This is how we learn to be afraid of things, even the most simple and mundane things and situations. Fear is as trainable as courage, and we are often socially conditioned to be afraid of certain things and situations. I have spent 16 years in tropical Southeast Asia, which has more frequent thunderstorms and lightning than almost anywhere else in the world.[8] My children never worried about the most intense thunder and lightning, because people in Malaysia are generally at peace with this daily aspect of life. Yet, I remember fearing ball lightning[9] when I was a little girl and would always close all doors and windows during the rain, even if there were hardly any thunderstorms in Estonia.

Fear is often socially conditioned, but fear in itself is not a problem. I am not asking you to get rid of your fear—that would be an extreme as bad as being paralysed with fear—but with more serious consequences to your life and safety. Being courageous doesn't mean having no fear, and it doesn't mean being reckless or risking your life for kicks.

Courage is about feeling the fear but still making the step into the unknown. Courage is about acting in spite of fear, with fear and through fear.

The stage is my natural habitat. It is a part of my office; it is in my work description; it is something I had to get used to more than 15 years ago. Sometimes I share the stage with amazing people, sometimes I am there alone, sometimes I get to prepare before I go on stage, and sometimes I find myself on stage out of the blue. I might be used to the stage, but I still have reverence and respect for it. I still feel the buzz in my body when I get on it, when the lights are on, all eyes and cameras are on me, and there is that moment of silence just before the first words leave my mouth. You might call it fear, but I call it excitement.[10]

I don't enjoy fear, and like many, I would prefer to have less fear in my life. But I don't like being on stage without it, without the excitement and the state of being alert and present. Biologically speaking, stress is your body's way to prepare you for what's coming—it activates your nervous system, your heart rate goes up, your senses are alert, your muscles tense, and you are ready to react to "the threat"—fight or flight—either way, you are prepared. I feel something similar when I am on stage. As unpleasant as it may be, I feel that the stage fright is what makes me 100 percent prepared to give my best to the audience.

The good news is that such tension and state of alertness do not last the whole time while I am on stage. Once I utter my first few sentences, once I get into the essence of the presentation, extreme stress subsides, and I start feeling the flow—that elusive state of genius. It's like being on that plane in front of the open door—once you get the kick in the back (initial intense stress), you are outside and start flying (state of flow).

The trick is the same-old "make the step into the unknown." The first step is the hardest and the most important. Once you are in the process, it becomes much, much easier.

And most importantly, don't overthink. Remember, your brain is out there to save you from danger. The only nuance is, there is no danger. The situation may be uncomfortable, unpleasant, and even painful, but usually not dangerous.

If you knew that everything would be okay, what would you like to try to do? Just play along a little and have fun!

There is one more important rule about courage that I would like to share before we move on. Your success is proportional to the size of your comfort zone. The bigger your comfort zone, the more potential for success you hold. The smaller your comfort zone, the less success you are capable of.

It is a very logical and simple rule. To achieve anything, you are very likely going to have to do something new, unfamiliar, maybe unpleasant or uncomfortable. Every time you do something new and unfamiliar, you venture outside your comfort zone. But the funny thing is, once you have done something new, it stops being unfamiliar, and your comfort zone has just expanded by this one thing you did.

I love this rule because it helps me dive into unpleasant but necessary things that do not have any intrinsic motivation in them. I remind myself that my success is as big as my comfort zone. I go to a dentist (and I'm really afraid of dentists), and I tell myself, "Kristina, you are expanding your comfort zone—it is an investment in your future success." I do the mundane and boring work tasks, which we all have to face from time to time, and I remind myself that this is an opportunity to expand my comfort zone and thus, invest into my future success.

It is a little arbitrary, of course, and maybe a little ritualistic, but it works for me. Whatever makes you take that first step into the unknown, go for it. Action is better than inaction. Movement is better than stagnation. But above all—you are safe—well, most of the time.

Reflection Points

I want to share a simple yet practical tool with you that will help you to be more courageous. This tool ties back to the previous part of the book—kindness. Self-kindness is an incredible fuel for courage. Here's your bravery tool:

Every time when you notice yourself being in doubt, worried, or afraid, pause for a moment and say these things to yourself:

- It is okay if I fail this.
- I can forgive myself if I fail this.
- I can still love and accept myself if I fail this.

CAN YOU
UNDO YOUR
Transformation?

*In some ways suffering ceases to be suffering at the moment
it finds a meaning, such as the meaning of a sacrifice.*

— VIKTOR FRANKL[11]

You are on a journey and, just like anyone who ventures out of the comfort of their home, you will need courage on this journey, but not to slay trolls, spiders, and dragons[12] (and I do hope you leave the last ones at peace). You will be a changed person, and as you change, you will discover yourself out of your comfort zone. In fact, for a while, your old familiar world and your cosy life may become outside your comfort zone because they belonged to the old version of you and don't gel well with the new version.

When I embarked on this journey some years ago, I was afraid of the truth, but more than anything, I was afraid of the inevitable changes in my perfect "Instagrammable" life. And I was afraid rightfully. I did, eventually, grab a sledgehammer and knock my beautiful Disney castle into pieces.

Did I ever doubt my decisions and choices? Did I ever regret having undone what took years to create? Did I ever want to turn back the clock and go back to my old life?

Of course I did! It would be a lie to pretend that you can jump out of a plane and not wonder at least for a moment how you ended up falling through the sky at a crazy speed. But did I really want to reverse my decisions?

All through his journey, Bilbo wanted his cosy armchair next to a fireplace and a cup of good tea. Yet, when he came back to his home in Hobbiton, he started plotting his own escape—this time, for good, never to come back again. Bilbo, of course, is a fictional character, but the illustration holds. People often romanticise their past, and partly, it is the fault of our patchy memory. We have positivity-bias about our memories of the past.[13] When you think about the past, your memory usually provides you with the best highlights—most joyful, pleasant, and happy moments are the most memorable. So you might think that you were blissfully happy before you embarked on the perilous journey of transformation, but something did push you onto that path. Can you bring back to your memory those moments of anguish and desperation? They are there, even if not as readily available as the happy moments.

There is always a great temptation to go back to the old and familiar life, partly because it is familiar and you have done it before, so there's nothing to fear. And partly because your memory of the past is unfair to your present, and the future—it is photoshopped into bliss while your present is clearly laid out right in front of you and your future is shrouded in uncertainty.

It is when you are faced with such temptation for the well-trodden path of your past when you will need your courage the most. Will you keep moving or will you turn back?

I once stumbled on a brilliant piece of fiction by Agatha Christie,[14] *Absent in the Spring,* which, in essence, describes a transformational journey of a very conventional woman, Joan. She is a perfect woman with a perfect life (sounds familiar?) stranded for a few days in a desert waiting for her train back home. At the beginning of the novel, Joan meets with an old friend who drops a casual, yet brilliant line: "If you'd nothing to think about but yourself for days and days, I wonder what you'd find out about yourself," and this is exactly how the story unfolds.

Joan is stranded in a desert for four days with nothing to do but amuse herself with her own thoughts, and in this time, she experiences a thorough awakening and transformation. But it wouldn't be Agatha Christie if the story didn't have a twist in the end.

By the time Joan comes back to London, she starts doubting her own revelations. Was it a hallucination? Madness? Joan steps back into her home and faces an agonising choice: Should she make a leap of faith into the new life, or stay comfortably in her old perfect world?

Can you undo your transformation? Can you ignore a moment of revelation? Can you close your eyes on your own awakening, transformation, growth pains, and slide back into your comfortable old world . . . and if you do go back to your old life, will it hold? Will you be as blissful in it as you used to be before you changed?

Have I been disappointed in my decisions? Yes, of course, there have been times that I have made a leap of faith, only to fall down on the floor without the support and the lift I was expecting. It was painful and frustrating. Have I regretted my choices? At times. But I'd rather regret something that I have done than wonder how life would have been had I taken a leap of faith.

I have had my share of regrets, disappointments, and pain I would have rather avoided. But then I remember that it is those regrets, disappointments, and pain that brought me here—I would not have been who I am if I didn't have those experiences. And paraphrasing Viktor Frankl's famous quote, pain ceases to be suffering once it finds meaning.

Reflection Points

Now is the time to take another moment for intro-spection. You can take out your journal and answer these questions:

- If I keep walking down this path and become flawesome, how am I going to change? How is my life going to change?

- What do I have to leave behind when I choose to live flawesomely? Am I willing to pay this price for the life on my own terms?

YOUR *Journey* BELONGS TO YOU

*When you say "yes" to others, make sure
you are not saying "no" to yourself.*

— PAULO COELHO[15]

Let's be super-practical and answer some pressing questions:
What needs to change in your life?
How are you going to communicate it to the world?
And finally, are you ready to hurt those you love? Because who are we kidding here—some of your choices will elicit very strong emotions and protests.

- Deciding that you have stagnated at your current job and that you endure it just to pay the bills is not the same as quitting this very job and letting your family know that now you don't have a steady income.

- Deciding that you are lonely in your marriage and your heart is starved of real intimacy and connection is not the same as proposing a divorce to your partner.

- Deciding that you deserve to be treated right and want your boundaries respected is not the same as having a hard conversation with someone you have been afraid of all your life.

The hardest part of living life by your own rules is making a choice between what is important to you and what your loved ones expect from you. Will you choose you? Or will you choose to please the people that you love?

When Vishen and I decided to separate, the hardest part was to communicate our decision to the family. It's bad enough to be disappointed, but it is a hundred times worse to disappoint people that you love.

Not surprisingly, our parents didn't take our decision well. My mom was beside herself. She was angry, furious, really, with both me and Vishen. I remember receiving a nerve-wracking call from my mom. I recall sitting in the backseat of my car on the way home from work. I even recall being stuck in a jam and the exact curve on the highway when my mom called. I felt frustrated because I thought that my mom misinterpreted the whole situation and was looking at it from the wrong angle.

I was about to start fighting from my corner when I paused and decided against the argument. My mom was reacting to the news of our separation the way that was natural to her and expected of her. It was her reaction, and it wasn't about me, Vishen, or our relationship. I could try fighting and arguing, hoping to sway my mom to see it the way I looked at it, but my chances were low. My mom was going through her journey, and there was no point trying to get her to take another path. She had the right to her journey.

And I had the right to mine. Part of my journey was to accept the fact that my mom did not accept some of my decisions in life. She wanted to convince me that I was wrong; I wanted to convince her that she was misunderstanding the situation—it was a familiar vicious cycle, which often spiralled into a big, nasty fight.

So I let it be. I told my mom that we could talk about it later when we were ready for a talk and not a verbal sparring. The next week was heavy. I didn't call my mom because I wasn't ready to hear her accusations without the need to defend my corner. My mom didn't call me either.

One week later, my mom called. She was ready to talk. She had gone through a week of thinking and digesting, and she had a revelation. My mom told me, "You know, I was so upset with you when I heard about your decision, but later I understood that I wasn't upset with you or your decision. I was upset with myself for not making hard decisions in my life, for choosing the status quo over my own happiness. When I realised that you are not wrong or crazy, you are just brave, I felt that I want to support you no matter how I feel about your decisions."

My mom had gone through her journey, without me meddling with it. And her journey was something that I needed too. I needed to hear these words at that time. They touched me so deeply, they gave me strength and confidence, and they taught me a very profound lesson: everyone has the right to their journey. And the best you can do is keep your light on, as long as you can.

Can you make a hard decision, knowing that your loved ones will disagree, refuse to accept, and fail to understand you? Knowing that your choice might send them off on their own journey and that they might not be ready to embark on it yet? Knowing that they may feel hurt in the process?

Do you have a moral obligation not to hurt your loved ones in such situations? Do you have to sacrifice your happiness for their benefit, to please them, to spare them the pain? Is it your obligation to make sure that your loved ones are not inconvenienced by your honesty and faithfulness to your values?

My mom said it best: she wasn't upset with my decision, but with her own past indecisions.

Nothing changed for my mom because of our decision. She still has me, my children, and even her "ex-son-in-law," whom she doesn't call an "ex," because in her world, he is a very current father of her grandchildren. We still hang out with both sets of our parents, go on trips together, and keep up the friendly and loving connection. It wasn't my choice that hurt my mom; it was her reaction to my choice, her mirror reflection—it was about her, not about me or Vishen, or anything else. And I am eternally grateful to my mom for vocalising this realisation to me and for giving me one of the most profound lessons in my life.

So is it a choice between your selfish whim versus your moral duty and responsibility? I don't think so. Your only moral duty and responsibility is to be happy and at peace with yourself, because this is your biggest gift to the world and no one else can do it for you. And this is what we are going to explore in the next section.

Reflection Points

Do you remember an earlier exercise from the chapter "Avoiding the Indecision Trap"? Let's take this exercise a little further. Let's play a game of pretending. Pretend that you know the right answer (even if you are wrong), what would you tell yourself:

- What choice would you make if you *did* know the right choice?

- What conversations would you have if you *did* know the right thing to say?

- What decision would you finally make if you *did* know that it was right?

You have an opportunity to practise real courage now—do the leap of faith—make that decision, have that conversation.

I have to give you a warning, of course: it can turn your life around, and it will be scary. So only do the leap of faith if it is safe. If you have reasons to worry about your safety, ask for help from a professional. Do not take unnecessary risks.

PART VIII

LIVING
flawesomely

A NEW
Life

You cannot help anyone if you are not happy.

— DALAI LAMA XIV[1]

Your only moral duty is to be happy and at peace with yourself. That is a bold declaration, and if it were taken out of context, it would be an invitation for harsh criticism.

I was 28 when I realised that not only was there nothing wrong with wanting to be happy, but there might be a possibility that prioritising my own happiness was not entirely immoral.

Before that memorable day, I remember staring at a small, old poster with a simple quote to that effect. And I was immovably convinced that my moral duty and obligation was to serve others, serve a bigger purpose, and serve grand ideas of changing the world.

Naturally, my choice of career reflected this belief: I wanted to work for society. I started my career working for the government, which was in line with my education and degree, but very soon I realised that the government is rather slow at solving society's problems, so I shifted into the nonprofit sector and later to the UN (which is even slower than an average government) and, finally, I set off to start my own charity.

Charity is a curious sphere, I must admit, filled with kind, idealistic, and unfortunately, unhappy people, often dedicating every last ounce of their mental and physical energy to "the cause." They are, of course, very noble causes, but they leave little space for the individual to deal with their own life.

I don't want to divert this conversation and plunge into a world I am very passionate about, the world I've dedicated the first decade of my adult life to, a world full of inefficiencies, distortions, guilt, and of course, a lot of good feelings as well. But I do want to share one important conclusion that I made for myself over all those years.

People don't like being on the receiving end of charity and, furthermore, despise mercy. They may need gratuitous help sometimes, but people of all kinds and sorts, even the most miserable and marginalised creatures have dignity and a keen sense of self. We may train people to accept and even expect and demand help on the basis of their status, whether it is your change that a homeless person on a street might feel entitled to or pocket money that your child expects on a regular basis, but this is not our natural state—it is a trained sense of entitlement. Let me illustrate this further.

In 2009, when I was visiting the small Achuar village of Tiinkias in the Amazon rainforest for the first time, they had just opened themselves up to tourists, and we were the first group to visit the community. Native Amazonian Achuar communities had lived in complete isolation from the outside world until the 1970s.

When we went to visit the village of Tiinkias, the women and children were still shy and unused to outsiders. They were hiding from the visitors, and only their men were pushing through with tourism plans to bring some income to their communities, communities that were used to living a natural lifestyle, yet had found themselves part of a confusing economic web of the world outside their native forest.

When we were leaving the village, we had some cash left over and wanted to leave it to the people as a tip. But the women protested and brought out their handicrafts, insisting that we not just leave money, but buy some of their products. Still uncorrupted by distorted perceptions of wealth and poverty, these simple people needed to know that what they received was what they actually earned with their own labour.

I had never seen such a sense of dignity and equality anywhere else in the world, in any other marginalised or vulnerable community in need of help. But whether these different communities are used to help or not, the desire to be an equal part of economic exchange is something that I keep noticing in the field of work, which we so mistakenly keep calling "charity."

Gradually, over years of working with various vulnerable communities, I came to a simple conclusion. The world would be so much more of a better place if, instead of giving to charity out of guilt and obligation, we did good out of a sense of justice, unity, equality, and our own level of abundance.

When it comes to humanity's biggest problems, we are not going to easily agree on which tasks should be solved as the first priority and, most importantly, how we are to solve them. But I am firm in my conviction that your first obligation is to be happy and at peace with yourself, and only then will you be fit to go out and actively make this world a better place. Simply put: don't give to ease your own pain; give to ease the pain of others. And just like in an aeroplane crisis, put on your own mask first, before you help those in your care.

That, of course, doesn't mean that sometimes giving your "last piece of bread" to ease the hunger of someone more miserable is not justified.[2] But such giving out of scarcity cannot be sustainable and does not elevate either the giver or the receiver. It is about survival. In other words, your own misery is not going to make this world any better. Your own misery is not going to make someone else less miserable. If misery is what you have, then misery is all you can afford to give, and when you give misery, it doesn't magically turn into abundance once it changes hands.

So I realised that wanting to be happy is not such a selfish goal after all. It took me another decade to move from this simple conceptual understanding to actually asking myself the questions: *What is it that I want? What will make me happy?*

Reflection Points

This will be a simple introspection exercise. I want you to write the answers to the following questions in your journal:

- What motivates you in your work or calling? Why are you doing what you are doing?

- What do you do besides your work? Do you have hobbies? Do you do philanthropy? Do you solve social problems? What motivates you in these activities?

- Do you enjoy your current professional and social activities? Would you like to change anything? Why?

Happiness
IS A SKILL

Happiness is one of the slowest ripening fruits in the Garden of Life, and, like all fruits, it must be grown.

— HELEN KELLER[3]

The world doesn't need your perfection. Neither does it need your sacrifice of personal well-being. What it needs is for you to be genuinely happy and at peace. It is important because it is when you are happy and at peace with yourself that you can offer the world the best of you. And thus, we come back to the same question: What makes you happy?

By now, you shouldn't be surprised by me telling you that it is not in my power to give you the answer. I can share some ideas to nudge you in the right direction, but, ultimately, it is in your heart where you find the answer to the question of what it means to be happy, for you.

Naturally, since I have studied, researched, and taught on the subject of happiness for several years now, I could expand this chapter to the size of another book. But that is not my intention, nor is it necessary. This book, which you are about to complete, is not really about happiness. Rather, it's about what you truly need first.

You.

It is about your path back to yourself.

And it just so happens that happiness is a natural consequence of rediscovering who you are. Happiness is a happy coincidence you'll encounter when you heal your relationship with yourself.

So I will not tell you what happiness is, as only you can provide your own, unique response to that question. (In fact, your homework for tonight will be to come up with a definition of your own personal brand of happiness.)

But what I can do, is tell you what happiness is *not*.

HAPPINESS IS NOT PERFECTION

Let's do a little mental experiment. I want you to remember a moment of complete bliss.

- Maybe you were witnessing breathtaking scenery, magnificent nature, when you couldn't help but stop and take it all in.

- Maybe you were looking at the face of someone you deeply love and seeing them present in that moment with you.

- Maybe you were laughing together with the most adorable children (and I am willing to bet that those children were your own).

I'm sure you have experienced such moments of complete bliss, and you must know how it feels. Recreate this moment right now—imagine it, feel the bliss, feel the joy.

Now ask yourself this question: How could you improve this moment and make it more perfect?

Feel weird answering this question?

I sure hope you do. I asked you this jarring question on purpose. The point I am trying to make is this: happy, joyful, blissful moments are perfect the way they are, exactly because they are blissful and happy.

In the words of one of our amazing Mindvalley teachers, business school professor, author, speaker, and wonderful human being, Srikumar Rao: "You are not happy because everything is perfect. Everything is perfect because you are happy."[4]

Happiness doesn't need perfection. In fact, perfectionism is a killer of happiness, because it comes with conditions and rules. For something to be perfect, that something has to tick off a lot of boxes and meet a lot of conditions. Yet it is the idea that you will be happy when a certain condition is met that prevents you from being happy instantaneously and in such circumstances as you presently have.

As professor Rao puts it (in my loose interpretation), you have to give up an "if . . . then . . ." definition of happiness. For example:

- If I lose weight, then I'll be happy.
- If I find the love of my life, then I'll be happy.
- If I earn a million dollars, then I'll be happy.

It is in the nature of human beings to be constantly striving toward something. Once you reach a certain goal, you set a new goal right away, and you barely take a moment to celebrate the one you have just achieved. So you set a new goal, then another one, then another one, and eventually, it becomes a maddening race for happiness dangling like a carrot on the end of the stick—always at arm's length, but never truly attainable.

HAPPINESS IS NOT AN EMOTION

Impermanence is in the nature of all emotions. Emotions are fluid and volatile. They change as you acknowledge and feel them, and as you express them.

It is obvious, then, that if you define happiness as an emotion, it is going to be elusive, never to stay for good.

Unfortunately, contemporary psychology doesn't have a good definition of happiness. It is often classified as an emotion or identified with a certain set of emotions, such as positive affectivity, unlike depression, for example, which is recognised as a state, even a medical diagnosis. I wish we were as loyal to the state of happiness as we are to chronic stress and depression.

We recognise that destructive states can be permanent, yet we insist that happiness is transient. You must have heard the idea: if you chase happiness, you will never attain it. Of course, you never would if you define it as an emotion, if you equate it to such feelings as joy, excitement, fun, euphoria, and pleasure—intense, enjoyable, but impermanent.

Let us turn things around a little bit. Let's give up the idea of happiness as an emotion paradigm and look at it as a certain resourceful state. A state is a much more stable condition. States are trainable, achievable, and can be maintained for an extended period of time.

I like the theory of hedonic adaptation, or the hedonic treadmill, proposed by Philip Brickman and Donald T. Campbell in a notable 1971 paper, "Hedonic Relativism and Planning the Good Society." [5] They talk about a certain "happiness set point," a relatively stable level of contentment, to which we inevitably return, despite whatever negative or positive events may happen to us.

This theory explains why people don't feel happier as they earn more money or achieve more goals. This is why some people stay optimistic, even if major negative events come to pass. According to this theory, your level of happiness doesn't depend so much on external events, as much as it depends on your "happiness set point."

Figuratively speaking, it works like a thermostat: If you set a certain temperature on a thermostat, it will respond to external fluctuations in temperature by heating or cooling the room—if you let in a cool breeze from outside, your thermostat will heat up the room, and if you stuff the room with lots of people and it becomes hot, your thermostat will switch on the cooling system to bring down the temperature to the set point.

If we follow this theory, then to become happier, we need to raise our set point of happiness, and here comes an important distinction: Emotions are easy to manipulate—take a walk, talk to a friend, party, have a drink, exercise—all these measures have an instant effect on your emotions (even if not all of them are equally good for your long-term health). I like to call them "instant gratification techniques" that make you feel better. It is much harder to manipulate a *state*—it requires patience and time, and a long-term strategy.

There are several long-term strategies for lifting your hedonic set point that I suggest in my course on happiness. It's called "7 Days to Happiness" (you can find it for free on my website or on Mindvalley.com). I will not go into any depth about the course in this book, but here's a short list of some of the techniques you can start with: gratitude, being present, forgiveness, emotional literacy, nurturing strong meaningful connections, self-love, altruism, and meaningful employment.

The main idea, though, is that happiness is not an emotion but a state, a set point, which you can train like a muscle. To train your happiness muscle, what you need is to shift your attention from instant gratification to long-term strategy. And now we come to the third important idea.

HAPPINESS IS NOT SECONDARY

What is the one thing that you wish for someone that you truly love?

Most of us regular mortals want our loved ones to be happy. In fact, we wish everyone happiness. This is how our social interaction is wired: we wish happy birthdays, happy anniversaries, happy holidays, and all sorts of happiness.

Yet, if you were to make a quick survey among your friends, you would likely discover that not one of them had personal happiness written down as a goal in their new year resolutions. In fact, it is a little uncomfortable to admit that you prioritise happiness enough to set it as a goal.

Unfortunately, our contemporary discourse on happiness is not making the topic any more fashionable. We keep seeing messages that happiness is not as important as success. We keep being bombarded with the instruction that we should not chase happiness. Furthermore, we shouldn't follow our heart, but rather should follow our head.

So is happiness important . . . or is it not?

I believe that happiness is of the greatest importance. But not only this: I believe that happiness must be actively trained as a skill. It is a little ironic that we tell each other to refrain from chasing happiness considering that one fundamental rule in personal growth is putting work into what you want to achieve.

If you want to have a beautiful, fit, and healthy body, you have to work on it. If you want to have a loving and deep connection with your partner, you have to work on your relationship. If you want to be rich, you have to work on your money mindset. If you want to build a business, you definitely have to work on it. So, why, tell me, do we think that if you want to be happy, you should *not* work on it?! Why do we expect it to spontaneously happen, out of the blue?

Unfortunately, we often take happiness as some kind of a prize at the end of a journey, or as a reward for a life well lived. And we hope that it will just happen organically, that we will, at some point, stumble upon it.

So, on one hand, we don't prioritise happiness; we reject the idea of cultivating and training it. But on the other hand, it's the only thing we secretly wish for ourselves and others.

You will do this world a great favour if you allow yourself to prioritise your own happiness.

And if you are still not ready to give yourself permission, then let me do it for you. You are allowed to be happy!

Reflection Points

Let's do a little spring cleaning in your happiness rituals. Please make a list of things that you do when you are stressed or in a bad mood and you want to cheer up. Anything goes, even a piece of chocolate or punching a cushion.

Next to each item on your list, write down if it is:

- an *instant gratification–type* of remedy: It makes you feel better right away, but its effect wears off quickly and doesn't make you better in the long run;

- a *long-term strategy-type* of remedy: It gives you a little relief, but its main effect is long-term, because it is sustainable and aims at solving the root of the problem.

If you find this distinction hard to make, just write if it is a healthy or an unhealthy way to make you feel better and if it is good or bad for you in the long run.

THE DANGERS OF
Trying
TOO HARD

Life is too important to be taken seriously.

— OSCAR WILDE[6]

I think I know what your inner Hermione is telling you right now: "It's all nice and pretty, but one must still work hard, put in sweat, blood and tears, achieve goals and be productive, and thus earn the right to be a happy and worthy individual."

The main reason why many people don't give themselves permission to be happy is this weird idea that you cannot be happy and productive at the same time. That you cannot be happy and serious (professional) at the same time. That you cannot prioritise your happiness and contribute to society simultaneously.

So let's talk about it for a moment. Do you really need to grind your teeth, sacrifice everything, and conquer yourself to achieve anything worthy in life? And can you think of happiness while you do that? My thesis is that life is not as gruelling as we are used to thinking. And there's space for ease and lightness, for happiness and enjoyment while you are climbing your Mount Olympus.

Speaking of pinnacles, do you know what makes the difference between a good professional and a true master?

I learned the difference through art and music. As a kid, I went to art school after my regular classes. I adored it—the theory, drawing, painting, and sculpture sessions. After a few years of serious practise and drilling, I could draw and paint really well—I learned the techniques and all the rules, and I practised and improved my hand. But I always believed that I was not talented or passionate enough to dedicate my whole life to art.

You might be tempted to say that more practise and dedication would have turned me into a master, if only I had dedicated the proverbial 10,000 hours[7] to my art. Well, I have actually dedicated more than that over the years, but I'm still just that: a professionally trained artist, not a master.

I learned the difference much later, in my mid-thirties when I started playing a harp. There is a beautiful harp-playing technique when you play a succession of arpeggios across several octaves, and it requires plucking the right strings in the right order very quickly. The only way to play arpeggios like that is to completely relax and trust your fingers to find the right strings without you putting any mental effort into the process. The moment you tense, your arpeggios stop flowing and you start sounding constricted and forced.

To play this technique, you need to practise it over and over again, make lots of mistakes, keep practising and . . . just let go and trust.

Let go and trust—this is what makes the difference. Both professionals and masters have to learn and practise their art, polish their skills and technique, but to become a true master, you need to learn to let go and trust yourself enough to create in the flow.

Letting go is a hard skill, especially for perfectionists with Hermione Syndrome (like me), because we like to be in control, we like to take charge and—oh boy!—do we take charge! We do this seamlessly, especially when something is important to us. But what many of us Hermiones do not realise is that the more important the task, the more we take charge and the more we tense, the more we remove ourselves from mastery and true genius.

Yes, we perform, we get results, but we do it through our iron will and lots of work. Yet people do not run on sacrifices and willpower—or, at least they don't run like that for the long-term.

But there is a difference between getting results and mastery. To become a genius in any given field, you need to let go and trust—yourself, others, the process, and the Universe itself. And even more importantly, you need to have a little fun, enjoy it, live it, breathe it. When your Good Girl takes over, she is in essence placing herself between you and your genius.

And what better project for a Good Girl to take on than your life? Life is such an important project, in all its aspects. It is so important that we try really, really hard to make it right, to live it well, to be happy and successful. We try so hard, that we end up getting in our own way.

If you want to become a master of the most important art of all—the art of living—you need but one skill. It is the hardest skill of all—the skill of letting go (and enjoying the ride). You need to let go all the way if you want to fly, rather than dangling on that bungee cord.

- I will not argue with the fact that you have to learn, practise, and work your way up to becoming professional. But then, you have to let go and have fun if you want to be a true master.

- First, you have to know what you want. And then, you have to let go of your goals so that the Universe can show you the way.

- Yes, you have to be daring, dream big, and be unapologetically unrealistic. And then, you have to let go of your dreams and be at peace with what actually is.

- And of course, you have to learn to love and care deeply. But then, in order for it to be true love and care, you have to let go and set your loved ones free.

So how do you learn to let go when it is your life and happiness at stake? How do you move out of your own way?

As a Good Girl and a perfectionist, I know the pain. I need to be in control. I need to put in my best effort to make things work. My natural inclination is the exact opposite of what is required of me when it's time to let go.

Here's how we keep negotiating with the Universe, trying to reconcile trust with the urge to control:

- Q: What do I need to do to let go?

  A: You do nothing—you just let go.

- Q: How do I do nothing?

  A: You resist your urge to "do," and you relax. You trust the process.

- Q: How do I know that I can trust the process?

  A: You cannot know. If you knew, it wouldn't be trusting, it would be knowing.

- Q: Don't I lose control if I surrender?

  A: Well, yes, that's what surrender means— giving up control.

I learned the skill of letting go in a very intimate way.

When I was delivering my first baby, I learned that the only natural way to relieve the pain was to relax, physically relax. It is not something that you associate with delivery, right? So, when the pain kicks in and you instinctively clench and start grinding your teeth, the right thing, and one of the hardest things to do is breathe, relax, and let go.

Life is full of contradictions. That physical experience was a great way for me to learn the lesson. Now, when I feel that I'm trying too hard in my daily life, literally clenching and tensing, I remind myself to breathe and relax.

And that is how you let go. There is nothing to drill, practise, or master—I'm sorry Good Boys and diligent little Hermiones. You just do what you do naturally when you are not in your own way—you take a step back. You breathe. You relax. And then, you keep dancing through your own beautiful happy life.

Reflection Points

Since this chapter is on letting go, it would be a little ironic if I gave you an exercise to practise the skill of letting go. So your task for today is, naturally, to let go.

Put aside this book and your journal. More importantly, put aside all worries and concerns. Relax. You can go for a walk, meditate, take a bath. Trust that your transformation is happening even when you are not trying . . . perhaps *especially* when you are not trying.

THE WORLD
IS YOUR
Reflection

Everyone is a mirror image of yourself—
your own thinking coming back at you.

— BYRON KATIE[8]

So how do you want your life to be? And do you need to change anything about it?

Oftentimes, people turn to personal growth and start looking for a teacher because they want to change something about their lives. And the question, "How does my life need to change?" is the dominating motive in their quest for transformation, enlightenment, and improvement.

We could whip out our diaries and start a deep and elaborate exercise of evaluating and reimagining your life in all possible areas, but that would take us in a very different direction from the main message of this book. Often, the biggest and most important changes do not need deep and complicated reflection.

I believe that you have the answer to this question within you already. We often mask our fear and insecurity behind the idea of indecision, pretending that we don't know the answer or the way out. But it is in there; that is why you are on this fork in the road in the first place. It is because you had the answer before the question even came to your mind. If there was no answer in you, you wouldn't be asking yourself what the right thing to do is.

I'll tell you something else—if you feel drawn to go into deep analysis of your entire life to improve its quality, don't bother. Solve that *one* mystery, admit that *one* truth, find the courage to untangle that *one* difficult puzzle, and the rest of the pieces will fall into place.

You do not need to pop that magic pill, nor buy whatever "they" are selling as an answer. What you need is the courage and kindness to face your fears and be honest with yourself. *Brutally* honest.

When I started questioning my life choices at around 40, the one thought that I was afraid of the most was the question of what I wanted and needed in a love relationship. I tried to change everything possible in my life without touching upon this one area that made me paralysed with fear. I was trying to compensate for not dealing with this one most fearful area of my life by sorting out everything else to near perfection.

I'm not saying that divorce was the right or the only solution to my big fearful problem, but I lacked the courage to face the truth for many years, until it became so pressing and so unbearable that there was no escaping it anymore. And so, naturally, when I finally couldn't pretend any longer that everything was fine, my reaction was near-on explosive, intense, and extreme because I had been bottling up my truth for so long.

The sooner you admit your truth and face your fears, the more pathways you leave for yourself to choose from and the more temperate your reaction will be. It is because we are content with the status quo for way too long, because we turn a blind eye, because we fake it in the hopes of making it, that we finally end up needing the leap of faith, into the unknown, into the abyss.

And so, it is now time to be completely honest with yourself: What are the changes that you need to make in your life? What are the hard conversations that you have to have? What are the scary decisions that you have to make? What are the brave steps that you have to take?

I have good news for you. these changes start with you. You might be intimidated by the thought of communicating your new boundaries, your new rules, your new desires to the outside world, but it will not be as hard as you might imagine, once you come to peace with yourself.

Let me explain.

I was once invited as a guest speaker on an interview hosted by a wonderful entrepreneur and podcaster—an idealist and a passionate young man. We had a short chat before the recording started, and my host shared that he was becoming increasingly frustrated with the world, society, and humankind in general. I could relate, since I had spent the first half of my career doing nonprofit and voluntary work with marginalised and vulnerable communities all over the world. I knew the feeling of helpless passion and being overwhelmed, the desire to make the world a better place, the willingness to do whatever it takes, and the intimidating realisation that humankind's problems are bigger than what one person can solve.

I still care deeply about our climate, politics, poverty, and wars, but there is a nuance—I do have faith in people now. Yes, those very people who have been making mistakes and stupid decisions, those very people who have brought on their own problems in the first place.

I have a very keen sense of justice, and it is easy to trigger my anger, but one thing has changed profoundly: I am at peace with the world, with the mess we are in, with humankind, and with all our vices. It may sound contradictory, but it is not quite so. You see, anger and frustration are natural reactions to external events, but one can still feel those emotions, and, fundamentally, be at peace (or at least come to peace). I choose to leave my decision-making to the moment when I come to peace with what is going on.

You don't deal with a problem at the same emotional level that has created the problem. You need that peace and calm to be able to look at the state of things impassionately and ask yourself, *What can I do to change it for the better?*

And thus, I have come to peace with the world, while still wanting to change it for the better in various ways. Furthermore, there is one curious correlation I have discovered over the years of my work in the personal growth and transformation industry—that the more at peace you are with yourself, the more at peace you are with the world too.

- If you can learn to love and accept yourself with all your imperfections, dragons, dents, and scratches, you can learn to love and accept other people with their imperfections too.

- If you can learn to accept your own quirks and oddities, you can learn to accept other people's quirks and oddities.

- If you can learn to be kind and compassionate to yourself, you can learn to be truly kind and compassionate to others.

It is often because we cannot accept ourselves fully that we have problems accepting others to the same degree. If you cannot live with your imperfections, you cannot accept other people's imperfections. If you hold yourself to a standard of perfection, you will hold other people to the same high, impossible-to-achieve standard.

Your relationship with the world is a reflection of your relationship with yourself. When you come to peace with your own truth, your own boundaries, your own wants and values, you will have the fortitude to communicate them to the rest of the world.

It is because you feel shame or guilt for prioritising yourself that it is so intimidating to voice your priorities to the world.

If you feel shame for wanting to be happy, then you, naturally, project the same attitude on the rest of the world—of course, others will shame you for being selfish and wanting to be happy. But if you are convinced that your happiness is important and valuable, then you will not budge just because a few people may misunderstand your intentions.

My relationship with the world is a litmus test of my relationship with myself. If I notice the pattern of being triggered or irritated by other people, I ask myself, "What is it in me that triggers and irritates me, why am I reacting this way?"

I remember once listening to a wonderful speaker, a very accomplished young lady, kind and sensitive, someone everyone adored. She was saying all the right things, almost as if we had been studying by the same textbooks, so I couldn't agree more with her message. But with wonder and amazement, I discovered that what I felt inside was not love, connection, and admiration, but quite the opposite—irritation and distrust.

I was tempted to explain my unpleasant feelings with some obvious attributes about the speaker, "Surely, something must be wrong with the speaker if I feel like this?"

But my relationship with the world is simply a reflection of my relationship with myself. So, a more productive question would have been, "Which of my own dragons are triggered by this speaker? What is it in this speaker that highlights something about me that I cannot accept?"

They say that beauty is in the eyes of the beholder. But so is the ugliness, the irritation, and the disgust.

That, of course, doesn't mean that we cannot notice things in other people that are alien to us, or that we do not feel in the moment. But you must have some experience on one side of the feeling or another (say, when it comes to jealousy, manipulation, or violence, you may have experienced it as a victim rather than a perpetrator) to be able to notice it.

Allow me to diverge momentarily to discuss something fascinating. Did you know that different cultures experience emotions differently?

Take jealousy, for example, a rather complex emotion that has been studied in various cultural and historical contexts. From anthropologist Margaret Mead studying Samoan communities in the 1920s to more recent research by Brooke Scelza studying Himba communities, it has been established that the experience of jealousy and our reaction to it is greatly influenced by the cultural and social context of the individual.

Apparently, people in more masculine and patriarchal societies[9] tend to experience more intense jealousy and react to the feeling more violently.

Moreover, some cultures have words for emotions that are not familiar to English speakers. For example, the Japanese concept of *mentsu*, which is similar to English *face* yet has a distinctly different connotation,[10] means that for a person outside Japanese cultural context it may be hard to understand the exact experience of "losing face."

Or let's take the somewhat more familiar emotion of nostalgia. In contemporary Western context, nostalgia is a warm, fuzzy, pleasant feeling. Some psychologists even suggest indulging in nostalgia to improve one's mood, as a practise for cultivating happiness.[11] But did you know that as recently as 100 years ago it was considered a serious psychological disorder, and the Swiss physician who coined the term *nostalgia* in 1688, Johannes Hofer, referred to it as a fatal disease?[12]

The point I am making is this: emotions are often socially conditioned, emulated, and learned, and your perception of emotions depends on your experience of them. You can never be sure if another person's happiness is exactly the same as yours, if another person's sadness is exactly the same as yours. What you see in other people is merely a reflection of your own experience.

As I was looking at that lovable, wise, but difficult speaker who was triggering all the "wrong" responses in me, I began to question why. Why was she triggering me so hard? What did that litmus test highlight in my own personality, my own values?

I went on to understand that the reason she was triggering me so much was that I could detect a sadness within her. And that sadness resonated with the sadness I also had lurking within myself.

I realised that I was afraid of my own darkness. I am a happiness teacher, after all. Happiness is my topic, my particular brand. So how can I be a good happiness teacher whilst harbouring despair? And so, since I could not accept it in myself, I was frustrated to see someone so comfortable and at peace with their own flavour of sadness.

We are often triggered by the characteristics and imperfections of other people that we reject within ourselves. It often feels like righteousness or just indignation, but is it really about another person? Is it ever about another person?

The answer is, probably not.

So what is it within you that you cannot come to peace with?

If I were at peace with my own darkness and sadness, they wouldn't bother me with other people either.

If you are at odds with the world, if it irritates and frustrates you, if it triggers you, it is because you have an internal conflict, and it is your internal conflict that needs solving. Once you come to peace with yourself, your relationship with the world will fall into place—you will be at peace with the world, and all its inhabitants, in all its expressions.

That, of course, doesn't mean that you wouldn't want to make it a better place. That's another hot topic—fixing the world. How should you go about doing it? And *should* you?

Reflection Points

This exercise is called "Picking up Red Flags." Think of a recent situation, or an interaction with someone, which has triggered you or evoked intense and unpleasant emotions. Ask yourself these questions and give them as honest an answer as you can:

- Why is this situation triggering me?

- What in this situation is triggering me? Is it pointing at some of my hidden qualities, values, wants, and desires that I refuse to accept?

- Is this situation triggering me because it is pointing at some behaviours, wants, and desires that I deny to myself?

- What would I want to do with these discoveries? Do I want to change myself? Or would I rather change my attitude to this issue?

NO ONE NEEDS
Fixing

This frightful evil can and does arise from an apparently good root, the desire to benefit the world and others . . .

— J. R. R. TOLKIEN[13]

Gandhi is often mistakenly credited for saying that you have to be the change that you want to see in the world.[14] There are several ways to understand this saying.

The more obvious one is that you have to be the brave one to make the change within yourself first and thus inspire others to follow. But I would like to give this idea a somewhat deeper and less obvious meaning—the only person you can truly change is yourself, and you should not attempt to change others, because that may very well be an act of violence.

I bet you never thought of a positive act of change inflicted upon others as an act of violence, but that is what it is in essence.

The Russian language demonstrates this perfectly in the saying "Причинить добро," which means, "inflicting good." But when we "cause" good, sometimes we actually end up causing more harm. Allow me to expand this idea.

I was brought up on the ideals of my country's (brutally violent) Soviet history, and we were taught that a good cause can justify bloodshed and the loss of innocent lives. That was a lingering ideal of my country until its last days in the USSR.

I don't think that the Soviet Union ever moved on from the revolution of 1918 and the barbaric murder of the entire Russian Imperial Romanov family, including small children and servants. Since then, we all came to understand that a "good" cause (i.e., the Soviet Union and creating a communist utopia) had the right to inflict unimaginable violence on anyone deemed to be an "enemy" of the state, including several of my great grandparents.

And that may be exactly why I so vehemently rebel against "inflicting good," tough love, and other acts of violence masquerading as being worthy enough causes to justify meanness, cruelty, and barbarity.

"But how can true goodness, true wisdom, and help be violent?" you may ask.

In my 20 years of working in the personal-growth and transformation industry, I have seen an abundance of proof of the idea that a person will change when they are ready for the change, not a moment before, no matter how hard you try to change them. I, too, have been dragged to events, given books, and introduced to teachers before "my time," only to be cynical, sarcastic, and disdainful toward ideas and teachings, which might have been right and useful, but were not timely for me.

If you give a person something useful, but do it at the wrong time, it becomes useless for them.

If you give a starved person food, they will benefit from it. Yet, if you give food to a full person, they will ignore it at best. Or they may overindulge in excess food, gain unnecessary calories, and the same thing which was good in the first case becomes harmful in the second.

The same analogy works for ideas, help, wisdom, and transformation—they are good when they are given at the right time and in the right circumstances. Else, they may be useless, ignored, scorned, disrespected, and even harmful.

As in any other industry, we too have unscrupulous and semi-professional teachers, authors, and influencers who set out to improve the world before they are ready (as teachers).

I have seen beautiful, transformative practises—which are incredibly powerful when done with a skilled professional—misapplied and unscrupulously conducted and thus causing harm to participants, rather than good. I have seen people left emotionally distraught and in pieces with no adequate help at hand to assist the victim of such misapplied practises to be "put back together." And in extreme cases, some teachers have shown such relentless resolve to push their students to the edge, that there have been actual physical injuries and even deaths at personal growth events.[15]

A person should not be forced into a transformation. It is violent, unfair, and damaging, but more than anything else—it is unethical.

Where do you draw the line between your vision of what is good for another person and their free will and right to their own journey?[16] It may not be obvious if you are looking at it from the perspective of your own desire to help someone see the truth, but imagine if you are on the receiving end of someone "inflicting good" on you.

When my mom first came to New York, she kept repeating—"Americans are normal people just like us. And 'they'[17] used to tell us that there is nothing human in Americans, no love, no goodness. That everything is just an economic transaction with these people!"

I know where such ideas were coming from. I was a Soviet child brought up and brainwashed by the system with the excuse of it being for my own benefit and the good of our society.

Almost every populist dictator and tyrant has uttered this phrase to his people: "You may have questions about my authority, but it is for your own benefit. The country will suffer without me." Child soldiers, cult followers, religious fanatics, and terrorists—in one way or another, they all have been fed the same message—*it is for your own good.*

These, of course, are extreme examples of institutionalised "good causing," where millions suffer for the benefit of a grand idea. And even if your well-meaning advice is not quite the same as the overwhelming control of the Soviet Union, the mechanics are often the same. It is the idea that you know better than the other person.

The only place where it makes sense, to a degree, is when we talk about underaged children in your care. But if you think that you know what is good for another able grownup better than they themselves, then you are very likely deluding yourself.

That, however, doesn't mean that:

- You cannot express your opinion about another person's actions or decisions, especially if your opinion is asked for and welcome.

- You cannot suggest the right cause of action to someone you love and care about.

- You cannot offer help, spontaneously and without an invitation.

But you cannot insist that your opinion, suggestions, advice, and help must be accepted. And you may rightfully protest that you cannot just simply stand by and see how a person that you love is making an obvious mistake. I agree—it is a hard experience for anyone. But your loved one has the right to their journey, to their mistakes, to their lessons, even if it is painful for them, and for you to witness it.

And so, against my own advice, I will advise you against giving people advice, unsolicited opinions, unwelcome criticism, and unappreciated help.

And you know what—you are welcome to ignore my advice and do as you please.

But I will leave you with this: no one needs fixing. Some people may need help, but they will come and ask for it when they are ready. They will find their teacher when they are ready. And it might not be you.

Reflection Points

Let's do a self-guided meditation.

Assume a comfortable position, close your eyes, take a deep breath, and as you exhale, relax your body and your mind.

Think of a situation where someone that you love, a friend or a family member, is doing something that you cannot agree with. Answer these questions:

- What would I prefer my loved one to do in this situation?

- Have I shared my point of view with this person?

- How did my loved one receive it? How does it make me feel?

- Why is it important for me that my loved one does as I think is right?

- What will happen if my loved one doesn't take my advice? How does it make me feel? Why does it make me feel this way?

- Is this situation about me?

- Can I love this person no matter what kind of decision they will make?

Conclusion

THERE ARE NO RECIPES IN LIFE

*Life is simple and deep, but we
make it shallow and complicated.*

— VEENA[1]

"So, what is your recipe for a happy life?" was the final
question of the interview. I had been invited to a morning show on an Estonian radio station. It was a beautiful
conversation, and the final question was probably meant
for me as a hint to give a bit of inspiration to the listeners.
Yet what could I have replied? I am pathologically honest,
I cannot throw out feel-good phrases and cheerful clichés
just to please someone—anyone, really. And so I gave the
only possible answer—what I really truly thought was the
case—that there is no recipe, there is no one-size-fits all,
happily-ever-after ending.

And if you do happen to come across a one-size-fits all,
happily-ever-after recipe for happiness, it is just as fictional
as the inscription on the dark, magical signpost in Russian
fairy tales.

Wouldn't it be beautiful, though, to have such a recipe? Or a tutorial for a happy, fulfilled, and successful life,
which would be given to us at birth. All we would have to
do is follow it systematically and get it down to a tee. As a

Good Girl and a perfectionist with Hermione Syndrome, I would definitely be spectacularly happy and successful, no doubt. I'm great at following orders.

But life doesn't operate like that. There are no checklists, no "to-do" and "not-to-do" lists to achieve true sustainable success, no tutorial for real happiness, no recipe for a model life. There's a lot of good (and bad) advice out there, but it is not always a good match for everyone's life circumstances. What works for some will not work for others. What works in certain circumstances, might not work in other circumstances. What works for you today, may be the exact opposite of what you need tomorrow.

If anything, life is spontaneous, unpredictable, unique, and ever-changing. Life is full of opposites and contradictions that beautifully coexist. Night follows the day, day follows night. Darkness follows the light and light follows the darkness. Spring follows winter and autumn follows summer. Death follows birth and birth follows death. And so it goes on in constant motion, eternally changing and shifting.

That is why people ask for a recipe—to deal with life's spontaneity, uncertainty, and contradictions, to bring order into the confusion. And it's totally understandable.

Yet it is our attempt at making uncertain things certain that creates complexity. When we try to simplify the model and come up with a how-to tutorial, we chase our own tails. So close, yet so far. When we think that we can prepare in advance for everything that life has in store for us, when we try to solve our problems before they even emerge, we delude ourselves. All of these attempts at taming and bridling life create more problems for you than ease.

And if searching for hacks, shortcuts, and foolproof rules wasn't silly enough, there is a curse in our industry—obstinate one-sidedness. We glorify everything that we

deem light and good, and, consequently, we demonise everything opposite of that—the dark and painful.
We overlook our flaws, and, therefore, we overlook our
flawesomeness.

As if, somehow, there can be only love without fear,
only hope without desperation, only joy without sadness,
only compassion without anger.

As if, somehow, anything painful and unpleasant is a
learned concept to be unlearned and eradicated.

As if, somehow, a utopian world of pure love, bliss, joy,
and light without a shadow of pain is possible.

And if we accept this utopian world as a possibility, how much would we actually want to be stuck in it?
Imagine an overexposed photograph with lots of light
and no shadows—it may look gloriously lit, but without
shadows, without depth, without perspective, it will feel
flat and two-dimensional. Flat, like a flatline on an ECG
machine—stone-cold dead.

Few know that you cannot numb emotions selectively.[2]
If you numb pain, you numb pleasure just as much. If you
numb sadness, you numb joy as well. If you numb fear,
you numb courage with it. Just like shadows and contrast
give texture, depth, perspective, and definition to a photograph, just like darkness gives meaning to light, so do we
need the duality in life—its opposites and contradictions.

Not only do we need this duality for contrast and definition, but it is truly the natural state of things. I like the way
American philosopher Ken Wilber explains this concept:

> Spirit is not the good half of the opposites, but
> the ground of all the opposites, and our 'salva-
> tion,' as it were, is not to find the good half of the
> dualism, but to find the Source of both halves of
> the dualism, for that is what we are in truth.[3]

Put simply, every opposite is birthed from the same source. And so, life must be embraced in its entirety, with both halves of duality, as a beautiful mix of the opposites.

If we accept the entirety of life, its contradictions, unpredictability, uncertainty, and spontaneity, then it becomes obvious that one cannot create a single recipe for a "perfect" life. Life is not about following a script, sticking to instructions, prescribing every next step. It is not a military march but rather a ballroom dance where life itself is your partner. You need to know the steps and rules of each particular dance, of course, but you will only be able to perform if you are in tune with your partner, if you follow the music and are aware of your surroundings.

As the world-renowned philosopher Alan Watts once said, life is a dance, not a destination.[4]

And you will accidentally stand on your partner's foot at times. You'll glide like a professional at others. You'll mess up the steps one day and nail them the next. It doesn't matter. Because that's what makes you flawesome.

And it's when we come to love, accept, and integrate our flawesomeness, our true selves, where the dance gets interesting, fun, and fulfilling. Studying for personal growth is like learning the steps and drilling your dance technique, but your dance is, and forever will be, uniquely yours. Uniquely flawesome.

Thank-Yous

When I started this journey, it was just me, my baby (the book), and the holy spirit (my inspiration). But as we moved along, wonderful people came into my life to support me and make this book a reality. And all through this long process, I kept telling myself that my goal is so meaningful, that the Universe has my back.

And it did. It gave me the people, the chances, the answers, the support, and the time I needed. So my first thank you goes to the *Universe*, which had my back.

Now, coming down to Earth, let me thank some wonderful humans who had my back.

My *mom*, for the first coffee she brought in every morning precisely at 7 o'clock with a silent reminder that it was time to wake up and sit down to my book. My *dad*, for brewing this coffee for me.

Mashu for reminding me about my worth, for having faith in me much before I had it, for having my back, for bringing clarity into my work and (not the least) for bringing champagne when we had reasons to celebrate.

My children, *Hayden* and *Eve*, my endless source of love, joy, and writing material: for keeping me sane and productive, for hugs, cuddles, and laughter, and just for them being themselves.

Vishen, for the many years we spent together, for dragging me to my first personal growth event, and for his unwavering support in everything that I do.

Thank you to *Jesper*, for all the support when I was alone, one-on-one, with my newly written manuscript, for taking my hand and guiding me from holding a manuscript to thinking "a book."

I have to pause dramatically before I move on to the next thank you . . . for *Amy* has been so much more than just my first editor! I loved working with you: your brilliancy, your humour, the time we spent together working and enjoying life. But more than anything, thank you for being the first person to love my book, for your kind comments, and for your unwavering support.

Thank you to *Michael*, for taking my book to a new level, for making me feel like a *real* writer. I grew and evolved as soon as we started working together, so thank you for the transformation. My gratitude also goes to *Profluent* team for all the work they had done.

Thank you to my publishers *Reid* and *Patty* for your trust in me and my book, but more than anything, for allowing me to be my obstinate quirky self. And my gratitude goes to the *Hay House* team for everything that you have done for my book-baby.

A special thank you goes to my editor, *Lisa*, for all the work and meticulous care that my manuscript has seen in your hands. But most of all, for pushing me to do better.

Thank you to *Natasha* for everything you have done (and keep doing) to make my work known, for believing in my message and having so much courage—it simply rubs off. And my gratitude to your team at *Natasha Zo PR* for being absolutely awesome.

Thank you to *Vishen, Marisha, Allison*, and my Mindvalley family for supporting me in launching and promoting the book.

A very special thank you to *Vic* for going deep into my content, for being curious, engaged, and not the least, for challenging me to be a better version of myself. I have grown so much thanks to you.

Thank you to *Anya* and *Denys* for making magic. I love you guys!

Thank you to all the people, partners, friends who have contributed to making this book a reality, promoting it, and supporting me along the way. It has truly been a huge collective effort, and I feel gratitude for everyone who has been involved in the process.

And the biggest thank you goes to *you*, the reader, for holding this book in your hands! A book becomes a real book when it finds its reader. And none of this could have happened without *you*.

Appendix

EXPANDED EMOTIONAL VOCABULARY

This chart contains approximately 300 names for different emotions. Use this chart as a simple reference tool to expand your emotional vocabulary and to pick more appropriate names for your daily emotions. It will help you to increase your emotional intelligence and to process your emotions better.

In the head of each column, you will find the most commonly used term for an emotion. Below the common term, you will find more nuanced terms for this emotion, roughly arranged from vague feelings to more intense sensations. Emotions in the chart are not arranged in terms of "good" or "bad," since I don't believe in such labeling of emotions. I tried to place them in the chart logically, arranging similar emotions close to each other. You will notice, however, that even "positive" or pleasant emotions will have some painful and dark nuances to them if taken to the extreme.

This chart is a work in progress and you are welcome to share your suggestions on how to expand and elaborate on this chart via e-mail info@kristinamand.com.

Expanded Emotional Vocabulary

APATHY
Aloof
Nonchalant
Detached
Disinterested
Unconcerned
Careless
Indifferent
Unmoved
Passive
Phlegmatic
Apathetic
Resigned
Insensitive
Unemotional
Unfeeling
Numb
Blank
Vacant
Lethargic
Listless

ABANDONMENT
Alone
Withdrawn
Detached
Lonely
Forsaken
Neglected
Abandoned
Deserted
Powerless
Helpless
Vulnerable
Unprotected
Defenseless

GUILT
Apologetic
Penitent
Contrite
Sorry
Regretful
Repentant
Remorseful
Guilty
Culpable
Wicked
Immoral
Sinful
Vile

GRIEF
Melancholy
Downcast
Dispiried
Despondent
Dejected
Deptressed
Sad
Sorrowful
Doleful
Crestfallen
Distressed
Miserable
Heartbroken
Grieving
Bereaved
Inconsolable
Anguished
Agonised
Suffering
Morbid
Mournful

SHAME
Self-conscious
Awkward
Vulnerable
Exposed
Inadequate
Discomfited
Embarrassed
Chagrined
Abashed
Ashamed
Morified
Humiliated
Ignominious
Dishonoured

FEAR
Cautious
Timid
Intimidated
Uneasy
Unnerved
Tense
Alarmed
Worried
Apprehensive
Agitated
Jittery
Nervous
Anxious
Frightened
Fearful
Panicy
Aghast
Terrified
Horrified
Hysterical
Terrorised

PRIDE
Smug
Vain
Pretentious
Pompous
Snobbish
Conceited
Proud
Selfish
Haughty
Scornful
Superior
Arrogant
Patronising
Dominating
Condescending
Contemptuous
Disdainful
Disgusted

ANGER
Displeased
Annoyed
Irritated
Vexed
Sulky
Bitter
Resentful
Frustrated
Exasperated
Angry
Indignant
Hostile
Furious
Wrathful
Outraged
Mad
Livid
Hateful
Aggressive
Spiteful
Vindictive
Vangeful

DESIRE

Inclined
Disposed
Willing
Wishful
Impulsive
Desirous
Greedy
Thirsty
Hungry
Craving
Yearning
Longing
Passionate
Ardent
Fervent
Vehement
Obsessed
Insatiable
Envious
Jealous

JOY

Pleased
Delighted
Glad
Joyous
Joyful
Cheerful
Merry
Gleeful
Buoyant
Optimistic
Happy
Blissful
Elated
Exuberant
Exhilarated
Exultant
Triumphant
Ecstatic
Euphoric

COURAGE

Encouraged
Empowered
Confident
Enthusiastic
Resolute
Determined
Tenacios
Undeterred
Unflinching
Adventurous
Daring
Gutsy
Bold
Brave
Courageous
Valiant
Fearless
Audacious
Rash
Brash
Reckless
Impetuous

LOVE

Cordial
Friendly
Tender
Affectionate
Fond
Caring
Compassionate
Loving
Adoring
Doting
Worshiping
Passionate
Romantic
Infatuated
Enamoured
Erotic
Ardent
Fervent
Obsessed

REASON

Aware
Alert
Attentive
Observant
Perceptive
Discerning
Conscious
Mindful
Insightful
Resourceful
Reasonable
Logical
Rational
Unbiased
Fair
Just
Objective
Open-minded

ACCEPTANCE

Complacent
Complaisant
Compliant
Obedient
Docile
Patient
Considerate
Conciliating
Forgiving
Sympathetic
Compassionate
Accepting
Open-minded
Tolerant
Respectful
Supportive
Embracing
Appreciative
Grateful

WONDER

Interested
Inquisitive
Curious
Engaged
Wondering
Marveling
Amazed
Astonished
Awed
Surprised
Puzzled
Confused
Bewildered
Apalled
Stunned
Shocked

PEACE

Calm
Tranquil
Serene
Content
Balanced
Harmonious
Congruous
Whole
Peaceful
Amiable
Affable
Benevolent
Yielding
Submissive

Endnotes

Let's Begin

1. There is a gentle nod to three of my favourite novelists in this introduction: Jane Austen, Charlotte Brontë, and J. R. R. Tolkien.

Part I: The Path Back to You

1. Rita Mae Brown, *Venus Envy* (New York: Bantam, 1993), 88.

2. Mikhail Bulgakov, *The Master and Margarita* (Switzerland: Grove Press, 1967).

3. Mandy Hale, *The Single Woman: Life, Love, and a Dash of Sass* (Nashville, TN: Thomas Nelson, 2013), 177.

4. This quote is attributed to Spanish surrealist artist Salvador Dalí, but I couldn't find the exact source.

5. Mariana Bockarova, Ph.D., "Fall in Love With a Person, Not an Idea," *Psychology Today*, March 29, 2019.

6. Vicki Baum, *Grand Hotel,* published in English in 1929.

7. Jeff Haden, "A Surprising Truth About the Misunderstood Relationship Between Happiness and Success," *Inc.*, May 12, 2021.

8. Mount Olympus is the highest mountain in Greece and was considered the home of gods in Greek mythology and the seat of the head god, Zeus. Hence, it is sometimes used as an allegorical pinnacle of success and achievement.

9. Marisa Peer, "Crash Course For Phenomenal Success," A-Fest talk, May 2015.

10. Lewis Carroll, *Through the Looking-Glass, and What Alice Found There, The Annotated Alice The Definitive Edition* (New York: W.W. Norton & Company, 1992), 165.

11. Interview with Liana Hakim on Mindvalley Mentoring.

12. Bravata, et al., "Prevalence, Predictors, and Treatment of Impostor Syndrome: A Systematic Review," *Journal of General Internal Medicine* 35, no. 4 (2020): 1252–1275, https://doi.org/10.1007/s11606-019-05364-1.

13. Lindblom, et al., "Burnout in the Working Population: Relations to Psychosocial Work Factors," *International Journal of Behavioral Medicine* 13, no. 1 (February 2006): 51–59.

14. Reticular Activating System (RAS) is a subsystem of reticular formation, a system of brainstem nuclei and neurons, and its primary function is maintaining behavioural arousal and consciousness. For the purpose of this book, I am considerably simplifying the explanation of its function.

15. Robert M. Yerkes and John D. Dodson, "The Relation of Strength of Stimulus to Rapidity of Habit Formation," *Journal of Comparative Neurology & Psychology*, 18, 459–482, 1908.

16. Alfie Kohn, "Do We Perform Better Under Pressure?" *Psychology Today*, December 18, 2017.

17. This quote is widely attributed to American business magnate and investor Warren Buffett and referenced in many reputable sources, including *Forbes* and *Inc.* magazines; however, I have not been able to locate the exact source of this quotation.

18. Steven Kotler is a *New York Times* best-selling author of *The Rise of Superman: Decoding the Science of Ultimate Human Performance*, an award-winning journalist, and the founder and executive director of the Flow Research Collective.

19. Steven Kotler, "Habit of Ferocity," Mindvalley Quest.

Part II: Finding Your Own Truth

1. Oscar Wilde, "Portrait of Mr. W.H.," *Blackwood's Magazine*, 1889.

2. A memory-erasing spell in the *Harry Potter* book series by J. K. Rowling, 1997–2007.

3. J. R. R. Tolkien, *The Hobbit, or There and Back Again* (London: G, Allin & Unwin, 1937).

4. Alfie Kohn, "Grit: A Skeptical Look at the Latest Educational Fad," AlfieKohn.com, Fall 2014, https://www.alfiekohn.org/article/grit/.

5. Popular personal growth training "Unleash the Power Within" by Tony Robbins, which is widely known for the Fire Walk ritual.

6. Robin Sharma, *The Monk Who Sold His Ferrari* (New York: HarperCollins, 1997).

7. Vipassana is an ancient Buddhist meditation technique focusing on mindfulness, and ashram is a spiritual hermitage or retreat in Indian religious tradition.

8. Deanna C. Friesen and Ellen Bialystok, "Metalinguistic Ability in Bilingual Children: The Role of Executive Control," *Rivista di psicolinguistica applicata* 12, no. 3 (2012): 47–56.

9. Evelyn Fogwe Chibaka, "Advantages of Bilingualism and Multilingualism: Multidimensional Research Findings," *Multilingualism and Bilingualism* (2018), https://doi.org/10.5772/intechopen.74625

10. Boaz Keysar, Sayuri L. Hayakawa, and Sun Gyu An, "The Foreign-Language Effect: Thinking in a Foreign Tongue Reduces Decision Biases," *Psychological Science* 23, no. 6 (April 18, 2012), https://doi.org/10.1177/09567976114321.

11. Elena Nicoladis, Dorothea Hui, and Sandra A. Wiebe, "Language Dominance and Cognitive Flexibility in French–English Bilingual Children," *Frontiers in Psychology* (September 7, 2018). https://doi.org/10.3389/fpsyg.2018.01697.

12. Richard Handler, "Authenticity," *Anthropology Today* 2, no. 1 (February 1986): 2–4.

13. Authenticity and similar phenomena, such as sincerity or congruency between emotions and their expression, have been studied by several philosophers, mostly as part of moral studies and ethics, but there is not much material to refer to, and there is little consensus on the definition of authenticity.

14. Brené Brown, "The Power of Vulnerability: Teachings of Authenticity, Connection, and Courage," filmed June 2010 Houston, Texas, TEDxHouston, https://www.ted.com/talks/brene_brown_the_power_of_vulnerability.

15. Brené Brown, *Dare to Lead* (New York: Random House, 2018).

16. Brené Brown, "The Power of Vulnerability."

17. Audre Lorde, *Sister Outsider: Essays and Speeches* (New York: Ten Speed Press, 1984).

18. Lewis Carroll, *The Annotated Alice. The Definitive Edition* (New York: W.W. Norton & Company, 1999), 66.

19. The original Blue Zones are the five regions around the world where a higher than usual number of people live much longer than the average life expectancy. You can study more about Blue Zones and their lessons in longevity here: https://www.bluezones.com/.

20. Ogilvy Paris, "Dove Inner Thoughts" commercial, June 2015.

Part III: Switching Off Autopilot

1. John Steinbeck, *East of Eden* (New York: Penguin Books, 2002).

2. Ovid, *Metamorphoses*, 8 AD, translated by John Dryden in 1717.

3. Eva M Krockow, "How Many Decisions Do We Make Each Day?," Psychology Today (Sussex Publishers, September 27, 2018), https://www.psychologytoday.com/us/blog/stretching-theory/201809/how-many-decisions-do-we-make-each-day. There is no good estimate of the exact number of decisions that we make every day, partially because there is no consensus on the definition of *decision* and partially because cognitive scientists have not seriously researched the topic. One of the most cited numbers—35, 000 decisions—has not been empirically proven, but it is clear that the actual number will be a few hundred or even thousands, and the vast majority of these decisions are made unconsciously.

4. Here, I am once again simplifying the main message, but if you are curious about a more scientific approach to my rather general statement, you can research "explanatory styles" and the effect of optimistic and pessimistic explanatory styles on the quality of life. There is plenty of research and empirical evidence to prove that optimistic thought patterns improve health, quality of life, and even productivity at work.

5. Michael Inzlicht and Malte Friese, "Willpower Is Overrated," *Behavioral and Brain Sciences* 44, (April 26, 2021), https://doi.org/10.1017/S0140525X20000795.

6. "What You Need to Know About Willpower: The Psychological Science of Self-Control," *American Psychological Association*, 2012,

https://www.apa.org/topics/personality/willpower. Some research shows that willpower, or self-control, can be depleted. Moreover, if you exert self-control in one area of your life, you will be less able to exercise willpower in other, unrelated areas.

7. Unless being in resistance is what you enjoy, which is possible. In that case, do what you enjoy, not what I recommend.

8. In financial investment, compounding means that an asset's earnings are reinvested to generate their own increased earnings.

9. This familiar quote has been attributed to many remarkable historical figures: Lao Tzu, Gautama Buddha, Ralph Waldo Emerson, and even Margaret Thatcher. But I am afraid that it is simply colloquial wisdom, which, in this particular form, was written down in an article by an entrepreneur, Frank Outlaw, in 1977.

10. Numerous research proves that intrinsic motivation leads to enhanced persistence, performance, and creativity, most notably studies by Edward L. Deci and Richard Ryan, the psychologists who empirically proved self-determination theory.

11. Albert Einstein, *Einstein's Essays in Science* (Mineola, NY: Dover, 2009).

12. Antoine de Saint-Exupéry, *The Little Prince* (London: Egmont, 2005).

Part IV: The Art of Imperfection

1. Gertrude Stein, *Everybody's Autobiography* (New York: Random House, 1937).

2. My use of the word *role* is consistent with role theory in social psychology, although I don't go into depth of how various roles influence our cognition and interaction with the world.

3. Romeo Vitelli, Ph.D., "When Does Lying Begin?," *Psychology Today*, November 11, 2013.

4. It is common knowledge in paediatrics, and paediatric psychologist Emily Mudd, Ph.D., addresses this: "We generally expect toddlers to experience some aggressive behaviours. At this stage, kids tend to resort to physical expressions of their frustration, simply because they don't yet have the language skills to express themselves." Cleveland Clinic, Nov. 2018.

5. According to behavioural psychologist Dr. Albert Mehrabian, in conveying attitudes and emotions, only 7 percent of communication is verbal, with tonality of voice comprising 38 percent and body language 55 percent of communication—which is his famous 7–38–55 percent rule.

6. Mark Waid, *Superman: Birthright* (DC Comics, 2003–2004).

7. According to Roy Baumeister and Mark Leary (1995), belongingness—the emotional need to belong to and be an accepted member of a group—is a fundamental human motivation. Abraham Maslow (1943) considered the need to belong as a major source of human motivation.

8. Brené Brown, "The Power of Vulnerability," TEDxHouston talk, June 2010, https://brenebrown.com/videos/ ted-talk-the-power-of-vulnerability/.

9. I must confess that I have not read the book *King of Thorns* by Mark Lawrence (2013), where this quote comes from, but I find its message brilliant, and I couldn't help using it as an opening for this chapter.

10. Alice H. Eagly and Steven J. Karau, "Role Congruity Theory of Prejudice Toward Female Leaders," *Psychological Review* 109, no. 3 (2002): 573–598.

11. This wonderful quote is attributed to Prof. Robert A. F. Thurman, an American Buddhist author and academic. Rodger Kamenetz, "Robert Thurman Doesn't Look Buddhist," *New York Times Magazine*, May 1996.

12. According to Wikipedia, "Cognitive dissonance is the perception of contradictory information," which causes stress and discomfort "when two actions or ideas are not psychologically consistent with each other . . . . The discomfort is triggered by the person's belief clashing with new information perceived, wherein the individual tries to find a way to resolve the contradiction to reduce their discomfort."

13. I think this book should be added to the mandatory school curriculum. Susan David gives the basics of emotional intelligence and dealing with painful and uncomfortable feelings, a crucial life skill, which most of us are missing.

14. Also known as "congenital insensitivity to pain," or CIP.

15. I've been told by my social media followers that Americans are not familiar with the term *paracetamol* and I should be using *acetaminophen* instead. I am, however, deliberately using European spelling, measurement units, and terms in my book to honour my roots, and providing endnotes when needed for extra explanation.

16. Neel Burton, *Hide and Seek: The Psychology of Self-Deception* (Oxford: Acheron Press, 2012).

17. In psychology, the difference between coping strategies and defence mechanisms is a little vague, but traditionally, it is considered that coping strategies are applied consciously, and defence mechanisms are often unconscious, and people are not aware that they react to a painful stimulus in a particular way.

18. If you find this topic interesting, Sigmund Freud came up with the idea of ego's defence mechanisms, and his daughter Anna Freud developed the theory. Later, several schools of psychology tried to classify and categorise defence mechanisms to make the idea more practical. I prefer Vaillant's take on the subject, although there are, clearly, a lot of overlaps between different schools.

19. George E. Vaillant, "Ego Mechanisms of Defense and Personality Psychopathology," *Journal of Abnormal Psychology*, 1994.

20. Danielle LaPorte, "Defining 'Spiritual bypassing.' Overused and misused but still . . . very useful," daniellelaporte.com.

21. This is not her real name.

22. John Welwood, "Human Nature, Buddha Nature. On Spiritual Bypassing, Relationship, and the Dharma," interview by Tina Fossella, *Tricycle: The Buddhist Review*, 2011.

23. Susan David, *Emotional Agility: Get Unstuck, Embrace Change, and Thrive in Work and Life* (New York: Avery, 2016).

24. Here I'm using the word *they* with a little sarcasm, but what I really mean is that modern society does not value emotional intelligence enough to make it a must-have skill, like literacy or mathematics.

25. Susan David is my personal favourite, but naturally, there are a lot of other great authors and amazing books on the topic.

26. I am referring to *bottling*—the process of suppressing your emotions.

27. Naturally, no one eats elephants. I don't think it's even legal. I'm using an elephant as a familiar idiom to illustrate the concept of something enormously big. It's an Italian idiom, I believe.

28. I'm giving you a generic chart (see Appendix), and you can find a variety of such charts online. However, if you are interested in this particular topic, Karla McLaren does a great job explaining nuances and intensity of various emotions.

29. The two most notable advocates of journaling are James Pennebaker, with a series of books and articles on the topic, and Julia Cameron, the author of *The Artist's Way*.

30. This quote is attributed to Søren Kierkegaard (1813–1855), the influential Danish philosopher and theologian.

31. In psychology, people with martyr complex choose to suffer or sacrifice their own interests for the sake of others because it feels good. It is also referred to as "victim complex," although the victim mentality is more passive. In relationships, a martyr complex is considered to be similar to codependency.

32. My father's grandparents and my mother's grandfather were killed by the Soviet military in the 1930s and 1940s for owning too much land and employing farm help. It was known as the process of *dekulakization* ("раскулачивание" Rus), political repression, including arrests, deportation, and executions of millions of *kulaks* (prosperous peasants) and their families.

33. George Bernard Shaw, *Man and Superman* (New York: Penguin Books, 1952).

34. This is not her real name.

35. Marianne Williamson, *A Return to Love: Reflections on the Principles of A Course in Miracles* (New York: HarperCollins, 1992).

36. Kamal Ravikant, *Love Yourself Like Your Life Depends on It* (New York: HarperOne, 2020).

37. Part V: Honesty

1. Lucy Maud Montgomery, Anne of Green Gables (New York: Penguin Publishing Group, 2013).

2. I am not using this phrase in its original meaning related to scientific revolutions, but rather in its contemporary, somewhat overused meaning of a profound change in the way you view the world.

3. While this quote is generally attributed to the 6th president of the United States, John Quincy Adams, I could not trace its exact origin.

4. *Lie to Me*, Season 1, 2009.

5. Did you know that other mammals are also capable of deceit? Chimpanzees and gorillas have been caught deceiving their peers or caregivers.

6. Judi Ketteler, "We Need to Do More Research on Honesty," *Scientific American*, September 20, 2020.

7. Pamela Meyer, "How to Spot a Liar," TED talk, July 2011, https://www.ted.com/talks/pamela_meyer_how_to_spot_a_liar.

8. Romeo Vitelli, Ph.D., "When Does Lying Begin?" *Psychology Today*, November 11, 2013.

9. Theodor Schaarschmidt, "The Art of Lying," *Scientific American*, July 11, 2018.

10. Daniel Kahneman, *Thinking Fast and Slow* (New York: Farrar, Strauss and Giroux, 2011).

11. Daniel Gilbert, *Stumbling on Happiness* (New York: Vintage Books, 2007).

12. In cognitive psychology, such mental shortcuts are called heuristics.

13. In cognitive psychology, this phenomenon is known as choice-supportive bias or post-purchase rationalisation.

14. Antoine de Saint-Exupéry, *Flight to Arras* (New York: Reynal & Hitchcock, 1942).

15. Now, if you are wondering about the seeming contradiction here with my opening chapter, where I claim that authenticity and honesty are binary, in other words absolute, then I have to draw your attention to the distinction between honesty and truth. Truth claims to be a fact, while honesty is mostly an intention. I go deeper into this distinction later in the chapter, but I want to be clear—honesty can be absolute, while truth is rarely absolute.

16. Steve Jobs, Stanford commencement address, June 2005.

17. One such example might be the idea that humans are the pinnacle of the animal kingdom, when, in reality, we might be the virus killing Earth's biodiversity and making it uninhabitable.

18. Vishen Lakhiani, "Be Extraordinary," Mindvalley quest.

19. I'm referring to the bending spoon scene in the sci-fi movie, *The Matrix*, 1999.

20. Don DeLillo, *Underworld* (New York: Scribner, 1997), 493.

21. David Bohm, *Collective Consciousness: Exploring the Hidden Source of the Social, Political, and Environmental Crises Facing Our World* (San Francisco, CA: HarperSanFrancisco: 1991).

22. In case it is still not 100 percent clear, you can control your expression of emotions, and your reaction to emotions, but not their occurrence.

23. I'm not referring to any particular movies here, but I do want to honour both Marvel and DC fans.

24. Think of Hiroshima, Nagasaki, and Chernobyl.

25. Think of antidepressants, sleeping pills, and opioids for chronic pain.

26. "Esther Perel ON: Finding Love & the Real Reason Couples Break Up," *Jay Shetty ON Podcast*, July 2021.

Part VI: Kindness

1. His Holiness Dalai Lama the 14th, from his visit to Capitol Hill, March 2014.

2. Hans Christian Andersen, "The Princess and the Pea," 1835.

3. You might ask if there is a kind and compassionate way to comment on someone's looks. I really don't think so, unless you work as a stylist. Comments about appearance are usually unsolicited and unwelcome, and do not serve the receiver.

4. In private conversations with Katerina, an energist, a wonderful teacher from Ukraine, and my dear friend.

5. I am obviously simplifying, but bear with me for the sake of this example.

6. Oscar Wilde, *An Ideal Husband*, 1893.

7. This quote is attributed to a *New York Times* best-selling author Alexandra Elle; however, I could not find the exact source.

Part VII: Courage

1. Pema Chödrön, *When Things Fall Apart*, (Boulder, CO: Shambhala, 1997).

2. Bertrand Russell, *The Conquest of Happiness* (New York: Liveright, 1930).

3. According to legends, the boulder reads: "Налево пойдешь—коня потеряешь, направо пойдешь—жизнь потеряешь, прямо пойдешь - жив будешь, да себя позабудешь." (Rus).

4. Roughly 12,000 feet, for those who operate in another system.

5. Eleanor Roosevelt, *You Learn By Living* (New York: Harper & Row, 1960).

6. Approximately 20–30 feet.

7. "У страха глаза велики" (Rus).

8. According to Vaisala's "2021 Annual Lightning Report," Malaysia is the 11th country in the world in terms of lightning density, with 54.14 events per km^2 per year, and Singapore is considered the lightning capital of the world with 163.8 events per km2 per year.

9. It is not scientifically proven that ball lightning exists.

10. An interesting (yet another anonymous) quote came to mind: "Fear is excitement without the breath." Remember to breathe when you are afraid.

11. Viktor Frankl, *Man's Search for Meaning* (Boston: Beacon Press, 2006), 113.

12. I'm referring to *The Hobbit* and Bilbo's adventures, of course.

13. Positive recollections of the past are also explained with "fading affect bias," which means that emotions associated with negative events fade away faster than emotions associated with positive experiences.

14. Agatha Christie is, of course, known for her murder mysteries, but she wrote other prose, and I am referring here to her series of non-crime fiction published under the pseudonym of Mary Westmacott.

15. Paulo Coelho on Twitter, @paulocoelho, March 5, 2014.

Part VIII: Living Flawesomely

1. His Holiness Dalai Lama the 14th, in answer to my question at a private audience in Calgary, Canada, October 2009.

2. I am using an allegorical piece of bread, of course, when I actually mean giving something you don't have enough of for your own needs, or giving out of scarcity.

3. Helen Keller, "The Simplest Way to Be Happy," *Home Magazine*, February 1933

4. Srikumar Rao, "The Quest for Personal Mastery," Mindvalley quest.

5. Donald T. Campbell and Philip Brickman, "Hedonic Relativism and Planning the Good Society," in *Adaptation-Level Theory: A Symposium* (New York: Academic Press, 1971), 287–302.

6. Oscar Wilde, *Lady Windermere's Fan*, 1893, paraphrased and popularised by G. K. Chesterton.

7. The idea that true masters require 10,000 hours of practise to attain their expert level was first suggested by famous Swedish psychologist Anders Ericsson in 1993, and later simplified and popularised by Malcolm Gladwell in his book *Outliers* in 2008. It is important to mention, though, that Ericsson's original research did not suggest that 10,000 hours of practise are absolutely necessary for mastery, and he disagreed with Gladwell's interpretation of his findings.

8. Byron Katie, *Loving What Is: Four Questions That Can Change Your Life* (New York: Harmony Books, 2002).

9. Stephen M. Croucher, et al., "Jealousy in Four Nations: A Cross-Cultural Analysis," *Communication Research Reports* 29, no. 4 (October 2012): 353–360.

10. Chun-Chi Lin and Susumu Yamaguchi, "Japanese Folk Concept of Mentsu: An Indigenous Approach From Psychological Perspectives," *Perspectives and Progress in Contemporary Cross-Cultural Psychology: Proceedings from the 17th International Congress of the International Association for Cross-Cultural Psychology*, 2008.

11. I am not suggesting this approach, though. I find nostalgia a rather dangerous emotion, which is often a companion of pessimism, apathy, and depression, since your attention is stuck in the past

and your outlook for the future seems to be bleak compared to the beautiful and romanticised past.

12. Carolyn Kiser Anspach, "Medical Dissertation on Nostalgia by Johannes Hofer, 1688," *Bulletin of the Institute of the History of Medicine* 2, No. 6 (August 1934): 376–391.

13. From a letter by J. R. R. Tolkien to Milton Waldman, 1951.

14. While Gandhi definitely had expressed ideas to that effect, the actual quote, "Be the change you want to see happen," belongs to educator Arleen Lorrance, who used the phrase in her 1972 book, *The Love Project.*

15. While this is not the only example, this article by Sara Sidner, ("Sweat Lodge Guru's Attempted Comeback Angers Victims," CNN, December 8, 2016) describes the situation quite accurately.

16. Naturally, I am not talking about the boundaries that are set by the legal system or our social responsibilities, such as not endangering ourselves and others.

17. "They" was what people called the government in the Soviet days.

Conclusion

1. My dear friend Veena Sidhu, an entrepreneur and a goddess, soul-sister of mine, says these words to me when I come over for a little venting session. I thought it fit to close my book with a quote by someone so dear to me.

2. This is a quote from Brené Brown's famous TED talk "The Power of Vulnerability": "You cannot selectively numb emotion. When we numb [painful emotions], we numb joy, we numb gratitude, we numb happiness."

3. Ken Wilber, *The Simple Feeling of Being: Embracing Your True Nature* (Boston, MA: Shambhala, 2011).

4. Alan Watts develops this theme in his famous Tao of Philosophy lecture series, "Learning the Human Game," 1965–1972.

ABOUT THE
Author

Kristina Mänd-Lakhiani is the co-founder of Mindvalley, the powerful life transformation platform with an ever-growing 20 million-strong following throughout the world. She is an entrepreneur, international speaker, artist, and philanthropist based in Estonia and the author of *Live by Your Own Rules* and *7 Days to Happiness*.

Kristina's online Mindvalley programmes have touched the lives of over 20,000 students by providing wisdom, life hacks, and healthy habit-building formulas curated and inspired by her 20 years in the personal growth industry. She has created life-changing content with some of the industry's leading authors, including Lisa Nichols, Michael B. Beckwith, Neale Donald Walsch, and many more.

Kristina began her career working in the Estonian government. At the pinnacle of her success, she made the decision to leave her high-level job, move across the Atlantic to New York, and start over—all in the name of love. Kristina married the man of her dreams and gave birth to two darling children.

In New York, Kristina and her then-husband, Vishen Lakhiani, co-founded personal growth platform Mindvalley, which went on to become the world's biggest mind, body, and spirit education platform.

While expanding Mindvalley into other regions of the world, such as the post-Soviet countries, Kristina found that there were many ups and downs in her journey, and in many cases, she found herself doing what so many of us do—living by someone else's rules.

Eventually, Kristina found herself again and discovered what she wanted from life. She now believes life is too important to be taken seriously, and lives in authenticity, by her own rules. She became unapologetically flawesome and has vowed to share just how she did it with the world.

https://kristinamand.com

HERE'S HOW TO ACCESS THE

Special Bonuses

THAT COME WITH THIS BOOK

Don't miss these essential tools! To get bonus materials, including free guided meditations and the companion course to this book, *10 Questions for Self-Love*, scan the QR code or visit: https://www.mindvalley.com/books/flawesome/resources.

Hay House Titles of Related Interest

YOU CAN HEAL YOUR LIFE, the movie,
starring Louise Hay & Friends
(available as an online streaming video)
www.hayhouse.com/louise-movie

THE SHIFT, the movie,
starring Dr. Wayne W. Dyer
(available as an online streaming video)
www.hayhouse.com/the-shift-movie

***

BLACK GIRL IN LOVE (WITH HERSELF): A Guide to Self-Love,
Healing, and Creating the Life You Truly Deserve, by Trey Anthony

F THE SHOULDS. DO THE WANTS.: Get Clear on Who You Are,
What You Want, and Why You Want It., by Tricia Huffman

GOOD VIBES, GOOD LIFE: How Self-Love is the Key
to Unlocking Your Greatness, by Vex King

HOW TO BE LOVE(D): Simple Truths for Going Easier on
Yourself, Embracing Imperfection & Loving Your Way
to a Better Life, by Humble the Poet

SUPER ATTRACTOR: Methods for Manifesting a Life beyond Your
Wildest Dreams, by Gabrielle Bernstein

All of the above are available at your local bookstore,
or may be ordered by contacting Hay House (see next page).

***

We hope you enjoyed this Hay House book. If you'd like to receive our online catalog featuring additional information on Hay House books and products, or if you'd like to find out more about the Hay Foundation, please contact:

Hay House, Inc., P.O. Box 5100, Carlsbad, CA 92018-5100
(760) 431-7695 or (800) 654-5126
(760) 431-6948 (fax) or (800) 650-5115 (fax)
www.hayhouse.com® • www.hayfoundation.org

———

Published in Australia by: Hay House Australia Pty. Ltd.,
18/36 Ralph St., Alexandria NSW 2015
Phone: 612-9669-4299 • *Fax:* 612-9669-4144
www.hayhouse.com.au

Published in the United Kingdom by: Hay House UK, Ltd.,
The Sixth Floor, Watson House, 54 Baker Street, London W1U 7BU
Phone: +44 (0)20 3927 7290 • *Fax:* +44 (0)20 3927 7291
www.hayhouse.co.uk

Published in India by: Hay House Publishers India,
Muskaan Complex, Plot No. 3, B-2, Vasant Kunj, New Delhi 110 070
Phone: 91-11-4176-1620 • *Fax:* 91-11-4176-1630
www.hayhouse.co.in

———

Access New Knowledge.
Anytime. Anywhere.

Learn and evolve at your own pace
with the world's leading experts.

www.hayhouseU.com